READING STRATEGIES

FOR COLLEGE AND BEYOND

Revised First Edition

Deborah J. Kellner

cognella
San Diego, CA

www.cognella.com 800.200.3908

CONTENTS

A Note to the Student

Reading college academic textbooks can be challenging for anybody. The strategies included in this packet are meant to aid in the comprehension of the text by breaking it down into a more manageable format. They help you stay engaged in the reading and guide you through the difficult material. You can use these strategies with ANY textbook! You will find some sample textbook pages at the end of each module in order to practice these strategies before you try them in your own textbook. As you complete these activities, you will discover that you not only understand the text better, but also remember the content more easily as you prepare for tests.

Good Advice from Other Students Who Have Used this Book

A combination of strategies works best.

After you are done reading, don't just put the book away, go review what you read.

Experiment with study habits.

If you turn the titles into questions, it gives you a purpose to read instead of rushing to get done.

It's easier to learn from general to specific, so skim through the chapter before you read it.

Keep asking yourself questions.

Practice with the strategies is necessary to master them.

Strategies keep you thinking about the text while reading.

The strategies work for a lot of textbooks.

Use whatever works for you.

Using the questions at the end of the book while you read is a good way to figure out what the main ideas are.

When you are organized and know what to look for, it's much easier to read, understand, and study.

While studying, be comfortable, but not too comfortable.

Don't push off work until the very last minute, causing more stress that is not necessary.

When you take time and actually take notes throughout the text, you learn a lot throughout the chapter.

Reading the textbooks assigned to you is actually very useful and important.

College courses take a lot of time outside of class and if you want to do well, you need to have time management to study and to stay focused.

The strategies make reading easier and they make it more interesting and understandable.

If you use the strategies with each chapter of your book, you will notice that the exam is really easy because you already will have reviewed using the strategies.

Getting an education and being successful means passing the classes, and passing the classes means being able to understand the material given. The strategies do help you understand the material!

Textbook Reading Strategy/
Goal Setting Log

After you have tried the strategy, fill in each box with the date. Make a specific goal for each strategy—how you intend to use the strategy. Comment on the effectiveness of your goal-how it might help you. Then comment on how you feel about the strategy, its use, your goal, etc.

Date	Strategy	Specific Goal	Effectiveness	Reflection
	Immediate Recall			
	Focused Reading			

Date	Strategy	Specific Goal	Effectiveness	Reflection
	Vocabulary Development			
	Structure Glance:			
	HIT: Headings, Ideas, Terms			
	NTA: Notes Text Analysis			

Date	Strategy	Specific Goal	Effectiveness	Reflection
	SQ3R			
	Highlighting and Margin Notes			
	Text Web Connection			
	CPG: Charts, Pictures, Graphs			

Date	Strategy	Specific Goal	Effectiveness	Reflection
	Outlining			
	Sidebar Summaries			
	Concept Mapping			
	Introduction Conclusion Breakdown			

Date	Strategy	Specific Goal	Effectiveness	Reflection
	Power Point Slides			
	Test Construction			
	Summarizing			
	Strategy Application			

Date	Strategy	Specific Goal	Effectiveness	Reflection
	Metacognition and Personal Application			
	Reader Process			
	Creative Strategy			
	Creative Strategy			

Date	Strategy	Specific Goal	Effectiveness	Reflection
	Creative Strategy			
	Creative Strategy			

Pre-Module Activities

1. Exploring Course Syllabi
2. Course Calendar
3. Course Calendar Reflection and Goal Setting
4. Textbook Preview and Reflection
5. General Reading Strategy Reflection

This pre-module activity is a bit different than the modules, as it is designed to **organize** and **introduce** you to important parts of your content course. There are **three activities** and **two written assignments** that go with this pre-module, and when you have completed all **five**, you have finished the pre-module.

Introduction

The purpose of this assignment is to **explore your planning skills, your personal general reading strategies, your textbook and the course syllabi** for this class and for one other content class. The **textbook preview** will help you get a sense of how content is presented, the structure the authors use to present information, and what kind of review/study aids are built into the text. The **course syllabus preview** will allow you to map out your entire course and keep track of due dates and exam dates.

Step-by-Step Strategy Descriptions

1. Exploring Course Syllabi

Being successful in college means having focus, a commitment to succeed, and a whole lot of persistence. It also means knowing when and how to work hard and knowing when and how to ask for help. If you believe that success in school is preparing you for success in life, you will need to have a serious approach and treat school like a profession. If school were your profession, what would the expectations be? In other words, if this were your job, what behaviors would be expected of you? List them here:

_____

_____

_____

_____

_____

_____

_____

_____

_____

Now complete the "exploring course syllabi" exercise as the first step in _____ establishing professionalism as a student. (A & B) _____

A. Exploring Course Syllabi

Your Name_____

Answer these questions using the syllabus from your **Reading course**.

1. What is the title of the class?
2. What is the name of the course?
3. Who is the professor?
4. How do you contact the professor?
5. What are your professor's office hours?
6. Where is your professor's mailbox located?
7. What is the name of the textbook used in the class?
8. What is the purpose of this class?
9. What do you need to purchase for the class?
10. What is the attendance policy?
11. How are the grades broken down—is it by percentages, or do you earn points, or????
12. What is the professor's policy on late work?
13. What is the professor's policy on absences and/or late arrivals?
14. When is your first reading assignment?
15. When is your first written assignment?
16. When is your first quiz?
17. When is your first test?
18. Is there a midterm?
19. Is there a final?
20. What do you need to do to earn an "A" in the course?
21. What do you need to do to earn a "B" in the course?

22. Where can you go to receive assistance with class materials?
23. If you were the professor of this class, what would you want your students to know about the class that isn't covered by the above questions?

B. Exploring Course Syllabi

Your Name_____

Answer these questions using the syllabus from your **content course. (Not your Reading course)**

1. What is the title of the class?
2. What is the name of the course?
3. Who is the professor?
4. How do you contact the professor?
5. What are your professor's office hours?
6. Where is your professor's mailbox located?
7. What is the name of the textbook used in the class?
8. What is the purpose of this class?
9. What do you need to purchase for the class?
10. What is the attendance policy?
11. How are the grades broken down—is it by percentages, or do you earn points, or????
12. What is the professor's policy on late work?
13. What is the professor's policy on absences and/or late arrivals?
14. When is your first reading assignment?
15. When is your first written assignment?
16. When is your first quiz?
17. When is your first test?
18. Is there a midterm?
19. Is there a final?
20. What do you need to do to earn an "A" in the course?
21. What do you need to do to earn a "B" in the course?
22. Where can you go to receive assistance with class materials?
23. If you were the professor of your declared class, what would you want your students to know about the class that isn't covered by the above questions?

2. Course Calendar

For this part of the module, you will need your **syllabus from another content class. Use a calendar or your own planner to write in when papers are due and when exams will be held—and anything else specified in your content class syllabus. You also need to make note of due dates for ALL other classes.** To get the most benefit from the syllabus preview, it is a good idea to print it out and refer to it when making study plans.

Fill in your planner/calendar now.

Course Calendar Reflection and Goal Setting:

Now that you have finished filling out your planner/calendar, reflect on all there is to do. Make some specific goals as you consider your planner and all there is to do. Write your reflection on the lines below:

_____

_____

_____

_____

_____

_____

_____

_____

_____

_____

_____

_____

_____

_____

_____

_____

_____

_____

_____

_____

_____

3. Textbook Preview

Directions: **Preview your textbook from your content course** by looking at its features and thinking about the purpose of each feature. There are two main sections of this table: [1] the features of the textbook in general, [2] the features of each chapter.

Title of textbook:_____

Does your textbook have this feature?	**Textbook Feature** Yes or no	Does your chapter have this feature?	**Chapter Feature** Yes or no
Author Information		Preview	
Preface		Questions	
Table of Contents		Photographs	
Chapter Notes		Charts	
Introduction		Key Words	
Preview		Chapter Glossary	
Appendix (or appendices)		Diagrams	
Glossary		Summary	
References		Links to other sources	
Subject Index		Practice test questions	
Name Index			
Credits			

In general, which parts of the textbook will be most useful to you?
Why?

_____

_____

_____

_____

_____

_____

_____

In general, which parts of the chapter will be most useful to you?
Why?

_____

_____

_____

_____

_____

_____

_____

_____

_____

_____

4. Textbook Preview Reflection

Write a 250 word analysis (minimum) of your content course textbook. Consider the following in your reflection:

How is this book similar to others you have used?
How does this book differ from others you have used?
In general, how are the chapters laid out (hint: each chapter is laid out in the same way in a textbook but every textbook differs in the way the chapter is laid out).
Describe chapter length. Describe other specific elements that are included.
Which parts of the chapter will be helpful to you? Explain.
Which parts of the chapter will be difficult for you? Explain.
What is your overall reaction to working with this text?
Identify your goals for using this text and how you intend to complete those goals.

5. General Reading Strategies Reflection

Reflect on your personal general reading strategies for textbooks. Write a 250-word analysis (minimum) of your past habits. Consider the following in your reflection:

Where and when do you usually do your reading of textbooks?
What particular reading strategies do you currently use?
What has worked well for you?
What are your strengths as a reader?
What are your weaknesses as a reader?
What difficulties have you encountered?
What particular distractions make it difficult for you to stay on task when reading?
What would you like help with?

BE SPECIFIC AND HONEST

Module 1

Immediate Recall

Introduction

Reading textbooks does not have to be a long boring activity. But, in order to make it more interesting, you need to have a goal in mind as to how you will proceed. This strategy is quick and easy. The goal here is to practice your concentration as you read, and to practice recalling the information immediately. The focus here is on **general understanding** of the text, not memorizing the details in the text.

> Developing expertise in reading requires concentration and active thinking.

You will be required to:
- Read
- Concentrate
- Remember
- Write

Step-by-Step Strategy Description:

You will need your text, a timer, paper and pencil **and** your complete concentration.

> Using a strategy when you read will give you authority over all your learning.

1) Decide on the pages to be read.
2) Preview the pages to be read.
3) Set a timer for 5 minutes.

4) Read with complete concentration for 5 minutes. Focus on **general ideas** (not the details).

5) Close the book.

6) Write in paragraph format what you remember.

Practice this several times at different sittings. When you believe that you have mastered your concentration and your comprehension for 5 minutes, stretch your time to 10 minutes, then 15 minutes, then 20 minutes.

Practice Immediate Recall below with the sample textbook pages that follow.

The more you practice reading, the better reader you become.

Immediate Recall : 5 minute practice

Write in paragraph format what you remember:

Immediate Recall : 10 minute practice

Write in paragraph format what you remember:

Immediate Recall : 10 minute practice

Write in paragraph format what you remember:

Sample Reading for Immediate Recall Practice

Almost a century ago, a Swiss psychologist named Claparede shook hands with a patient suffering from Korsakoff's disorder, which produces amnesia for recent events. Claparede had concealed a pin between his fingers, which pricked the patient as their hands clasped. At their next meeting, the patient had no memory of having met Claparede, but she found herself inexplicably unwilling to shake his hand (Coley, 1991). What the patient knew (that the good doctor was not so good) and what she knew *consciously* (that she was meeting a doctor, whom she need not fear) were two very different things.

Amnesics are not the only people who can respond to a stimulus at different levels of consciousness. As we shall see, we all do, but the signs are often more subtle. We begin this chapter by discussing the nature and functions of consciousness, examining the way attention focuses consciousness at any given time on a narrow subset of the thoughts and feelings of which a person could be aware. We then examine multiple perspectives on consciousness and explore the neural basis of consciousness. The remainder of the chapter is devoted to **states of consciousness**—qualitatively different patterns of subjective experience, including ways of experiencing both internal and external events. We start with the most basic distinction, between waking and sleeping, exploring the stages of sleep and the nature of dreaming. We conclude by examining several altered states of consciousness—deviations from the normal waking state—including meditation, religious experiences, hypnosis, and drug-induced states.

The Nature of Consciousness

Consciousness, the subjective awareness of mental events, may be easier to describe than to define. William James (1890) viewed consciousness as a constantly moving stream or thoughts, feelings, and perceptions. Shutting off consciousness in this sense is probably impossible, as anyone knows who has ever tried to "stop thinking" to escape insomnia. Following in the footsteps of the French philosopher Rene Descartes, who offered the famous proposition *"cogito* *ergo sum"* (I think, therefore I am), James also emphasized a second aspect of consciousness, the consciousness of self. James argued that part of being conscious of any particular thought is a simultaneous awareness of oneself as the author or owner of it.

Functions of Consciousness

Why do people have consciousness at all? Two of its functions are readily apparent: Consciousness monitors the self and the environment and controls thought and behavior (Kihlstrom, 1987). *Consciousness as a monitor* is analogous to a continuously moving video camera, surveying potentially significant perceptions, thoughts, emotions, goals, and problem-solving strategies. The *control function of consciousness* allows people to initiate and terminate thought and behavior in order to attain goals. People often rehearse scenarios in their minds, such as asking for a raise or confronting a disloyal friend. Consciousness is frequently engaged when people choose between competing strategies for solving a problem (Mandler & Nakamura, 1987).

These two functions of consciousness—monitoring and controlling—are intertwined, since consciousness monitors inner and outer experience in order to prevent and solve problems. For example, consciousness often "steps in" when automatized processes (procedural knowledge) are not successful. In this sense, consciousness is like the inspector in a garment factory: It does not make the product, but it checks to make sure the product is made correctly. If it finds an imperfection, it institutes a remedy (Gilbert, 1989, p. 206). In typing this sentence, for example, I paid no conscious attention to the keys on my terminal, but when I made a mistake—hitting an "m" instead of a comma, the adjacent key—I looked at the keys and corrected the error.

From an evolutionary standpoint, consciousness probably evolved as a mechanism for directing behavior in adaptive ways that was superimposed on more primitive psychological processes such as conditioning (Reber, 1992). Indeed, William James was heavily influenced by Darwin, and he explained consciousness in terms of its function: fostering adaptation. Consciousness is often "grabbed" by things that are unexpected, unusual, or contrary to expectations—precisely the things that could affect well-being or survival. Much of the time people respond automatically to the environment, learning and processing information without conscious awareness. Important choices, however, require more consideration, and consciousness permits heightened reflection on significant events and the likely consequences of alternative choices.

Interim summary: Consciousness refers to the subjective awareness of mental events. States of consciousness are qualitatively different patterns of subjective experience, including ways of experiencing both internal and external events. Consciousness plays at least two functions: monitoring the self and the environment and controlling thought and behavior. Consciousness probably evolved as a mechanism for directing behavior in adaptive ways that was superimposed on more primitive psychological processes that today continue outside awareness.

Consciousness and Attention

At any given time, people are dimly aware of much more than what is conscious. For example, while reading the newspaper a person may have some vague awareness of the radiator clanking, voices in the next room, and the smell of breakfast cooking, although none of these is at the center of awareness or consciousness. At some point, however, certain olfactory sensations may unconsciously be given enough perceptual meaning (smoke or danger) to shift attention. Paradoxically, the monitoring and controlling functions of consciousness are thus to a considerable degree regulated *outside* of consciousness, by unconscious or implicit attentional mechanisms that focus conscious awareness.

Attention

Attention refers to the process of focusing conscious awareness, providing heightened sensitivity to a limited range of experience requiring more expensive information processing. *Selection*—of a particular object, a train of thought, or a location in space at which something important might be happening—is the essence of attention (Rees et al., 1997). Attention is generally guided by some combination of external stimulation—which naturally leads us to focus on relevant sensory information—and activated goals—which lead us to attend to thoughts, feelings, or stimuli relevant to obtaining them.

Filtering In and Filtering Out Some psychologists have likened attention to a filtering process through which only more important information passes (Broadbent, 1958). For example, people frequently become so engrossed in conversation with one person that they tune out all the other conversations in the room—an important skill at a loud party. However, if they hear someone mention their name across the room, they may suddenly look up and focus attention on the person who has just spoken the magic word. This phenomenon, called the *cocktail party phenomenon* (Cherry, 1953), suggests that we implicitly process much more information than reaches consciousness.

On the other hand, people also sometimes divert attention from information that may be relevant but emotionally upsetting, a process called selective inattention. This can be highly adaptive, as when students divert their attention from the anxiety of taking a test to the task itself. It can also be maladaptive, as when people ignore something as small as a darkening birthmark on the arm or as global as nuclear proliferation and hence fail to devote adequate cognitive resources to them (Lifton, 1980).

Components of Attention Attention actually consists of at least three functions: *orienting* to sensory stimuli, *controlling the contents* of consciousness and voluntary behavior, *and maintaining alertness* (see Posner, 1995). Different neural networks (using different neurotransmitter systems) appear to be involved in these three functions (Robbins, 1997). Orienting, which has been studied most extensively in the visual system (Rafal & Robertson, 1995), involves turning sensory organs such as the eyes and ears toward a stimulus. It also involves spreading extra activation to the parts of the cortex that are processing information about the stimulus and probably inhibiting activation of others. When we attend to a stimulus, such as a mosquito buzzing around the room, the brain uses the same circuits it normally uses to process information that is not the focus of attention. For example, watching the mosquito leads to activation of the "what" and "where" visual pathways in the occipital, temporal, and parietal lobes. Attention enhances processing at those cortical locations as soon as a person (or monkey) has been signaled to watch or listen for particular stimuli or stimuli in a specific location. Recent PET data suggest that attentional mechanisms may generally increase the activation of a particular region of the brain when a person or monkey is signaled to watch for a stimulus; attentional mechanisms may also spread extra activation to objects once detected so they can be examined more carefully (Rees et al., 1997).

Controlling the contents of consciousness (such as deciding how much to listen to something someone is saying) and controlling voluntary behavior involve different neural pathways than orienting to stimuli. These "executive" control functions typically involve areas of the frontal lobes and basal ganglia, which are known to be involved in thought, movement, and self-control. In contrast, orienting to stimuli tends to require the involvement of neural circuits in the midbrain (such as the superior colliculus, which helps control eye movements), thalamus (which directs attention to particular sensory systems), and parietal lobes (which, among other functions, direct attention to particular locations).

Maintaining alertness is crucial in tasks ranging from paying attention to items on a test—and ignoring distractions such as anxiety or the sounds of traffic outside—to staying alert enough to notice a small change while keeping an eye on a radar screen for hours. A whole network of neurons from the reticular formation (which is involved in regulating states of alertness) through the frontal lobes appear to regulate alertness (Posner, 1995).

Divided Attention

Everyone has had the experience of trying to pay attention to too many things at once—and consequently not understanding or competently performing any of them. Psychologists have tried to determine the extent to which people can split attention between two complex tasks, such as following two conversations simultaneously; this is known as divided attention (see Craik et al., 1996). One way researchers study divided attention is through dichotic listening tasks (Figure 9.1): Subjects are fitted with earphones, and different information is directed into each ear simultaneously. They are instructed to attend only to the information from one ear by repeating aloud what they hear in that ear for a period of time, a process called *shadowing*. Attending to one channel or the other is difficult at first; it is easier if the two channels differ in topic, voice pitch, and so forth (Hirst, 1986).

Subjects can become so adept at shadowing that they are completely unable to recognize information in the unattended channel, performing no better than chance when asked whether a word presented in the unattended channel had been presented. Nevertheless, the information does appear to be processed to some degree, much as the smell of smoke is processed while reading a newspaper. This has been clearly demonstrated in research on priming [...], the process by which exposure to a stimulus (such as a word) affects performance on tasks involving related stimuli (Nisbett & Wilson, 1977; Schacter, 1992). For example, a subject who hears "England" in the unattended channel may have no recollection of having heard the name of any country. When compared to a control subject who has not been similarly primed, however, the individual is more likely to say "London" if asked to name a capital city, and he will more quickly fill in the missing letters when asked for the name of a city when presented with

LO_ _ _ N.

The data from many dichotic listening studies of divided attention actually suggest that subjects may not be dividing their attention at all: Failing to show recognition memory for the prime suggests that participants never consciously attended to it. In other cases, however, people do appear to divide their attention, performing two complex tasks simultaneously. Listening to a lecture while taking notes requires a student to hear and process one idea while simultaneously writing, and even paraphrasing, a previous idea or sentence. This is remarkable because both tasks are verbal and the content of each is highly similar; hence, one would expect heavy interference between the two. Psychologists have even trained subjects to take dictation while reading (Spelke et al., 1976).

Sometimes people accomplish such feats by rapidly shifting attention back and forth between the two tasks. Much of the time, however, people solve attentional dilemmas by automatizing one task or the other [...]. Automatization develops through practice, as actions previously performed with deliberate conscious effort are eventually processed automatically. While students listen to a lecture, their primary focus of consciousness is on the lecturer's current words, while a largely automatic process, perhaps drawing on some subset of attentional processes, allows note taking. Precisely how much consciousness is involved in divided attention is not well understood. Students can generally recount what they have just written even while listening to a lecture, suggesting *some* involvement of conscious attention, although their primary allocation of attentional resources is to the lecturer.

General Reading Strategy Exercise

Most students have difficulty with concentration and are easily distracted, particularly when reading textbooks. Identify all your distractions. Think about all the interruptions and all the times your concentration breaks down. Make a list of all the factors that prevent you from getting the most out of a reading assignment.

Factors

I can't concentrate because:

Now review your list and label.

Categorize your distractions as either: **Environmental, Physical, or Psychological** Label each distraction. Is there a pattern for you? Make a list of solutions to your distractions.

Your Text

Now practice immediate recall with your content textbook.

Then reflect on how this strategy worked for you.

CHAPTER: **PAGES:**

Immediate Recall Reflection

Active thinking and complete concentration is necessary for recalling information after reading. This is an 'after the reading' activity to check your comprehension and recall.

Write in paragraph format what you thought of this strategy.

What did you learn about yourself as a reader?

What did you learn about your ability to concentrate?

Was this an effective strategy for you? Why or Why not?

How will you use this strategy again?

What modifications, if any, will you make?

Content Course Reflection

Write a 250 word analysis (minimum) of your content course. Consider the following in your reflection:

How many students are in your class?

How often and where does your class meet? lab, lecture hall, classroom, describe size of room etc.

What teaching style does your professor use? lecture, small group activity, etc.

What aids does your professor offer to help you prepare for tests?

What types of assignments are given? Grading policy? Attendance policy?

What is your plan of action?

Module 2

General Reading Strategies and Focused Reading

Introduction

This module **focuses on general reading strategies** that you can use on an ongoing basis. It also introduces a strategy that you have, most likely, used many times before. It is called **focused reading** because it helps you stay focused as you read. For any type of reading, it is useful to know what you are looking for before you begin reading. For example, if you are looking up someone's phone number, you begin to scroll for their name because you know it will lead to finding their phone number. In much the same way, if you are looking for answers to particular questions in your textbook, you will scan the text to determine where to read it more closely. Once you have found the answer, you read it for understanding to be sure you have found what you are looking for.

> Establishing reading routines will provide reassurance leading to success.

General Reading Strategies: Some Things to Think About

[1] Time, Place, and Perspective

Different students read more effectively at different times, and in different circumstances. It is a good idea to start keeping track of how you study and learn best. With that in mind, these are some general suggestions that work for many students:

A. **Be an active reader**. Read with a pencil in hand, focusing on connecting the information in the textbook with your professor's lectures, with different things you have read, with other things you know about the topic.
B. **Review what you have read at different intervals**. Every page or so, stop and quickly tell yourself what that section was about. If you don't know or can't remember, refocus and reread.

C. **Get comfortable**. You can't concentrate if you are too hot or too cold, hungry, if there's not enough light, and so on.

D. **But don't get too comfortable**. If you are so comfortable that you fall asleep, you are defeating the purpose of studying. Textbook reading is still work—you need to approach with a purpose and a desire to get something out of it.

E. **Don't work where you are easily distracted**. Roommate, TV, stereo, cell phone, computer, etc. If it helps to have music on to drown out other noises, then that's a good idea. But if you find yourself singing along, that solution has now become a distraction.

F. **Find what works for you**. As you move through the course, note what works—and what does not work for you while you read your textbook.

G. **Focus on your purpose**. Why are you reading that particular chapter? What do you need to accomplish? This should play a part in *how* you read it. The next strategy, *Focused Reading*, may help you organize your thoughts.

> Focused reading provides a guide to help you apply the content of the chapter.

[2] Focused reading

This is a strategy that you can think of as a formalization of the **minimum of concentrated effort** one needs to do when reading a textbook chapter. Essentially, it involves identifying, before you begin reading, the **purpose** of reading the chapter, the **ideas** you are trying to find out, and the **questions** you want to answer. By doing this, you read for a purpose, to answer questions, instead of simply moving aimlessly through the text.

Step-by-Step Strategy Description

Directions for Focused Reading

1. **Decide what you are trying to find out from the chapter before you begin reading.** For example, things the professor has said to look for in the chapter, questions from the end of the chapter you need to answer, or simply things that you are curious about or don't understand that should be explained in the chapter. What your questions are will vary for each person and for each chapter. **If you don't know where else to start, begin by looking for questions at the end of the chapter**. When you have come up with questions or items you want to find the answer for, write them down, either on a piece of paper, in the margins of your textbook, or on a chart.

2. **After you have identified some questions you want to answer, begin reading the chapter**. As you come across the answer to your question (or an area that informs you about the question) write the answer down, and note *where* in the text you found it.

3. After you finish the chapter and are reviewing for a test, read your questions again, and try to answer them. For any question you can not answer, flip to the section you have noted and re-read that section.

It may help to think about focused reading in terms of a chart. By making a chart like the sample below, you are also making a study guide.

Focused Questions:		Answer to the question, and where in the reading you found information about your focused question: (page #, paragraph, etc.)
Concept/Question 1:		
Concept/Question 2:		
Concept/Question 3:		

Using the Sample Reading that follows, try the strategy on the practice textbook excerpt.
*Know before you read what you are trying to find out. For example, are there **questions** in the text you are trying to answer? If so, read those questions first, write them in the column below, and keep them in the back of your mind while you read the text. When you get to something in the text that has to do with the question, make a note of where you found that information in the column to the right. Or, for another example, are you expecting to find a particular **concept or idea** in the text? If so, write that concept down and make a note of where you find information in the text that involves that concept.*

Focused Questions:		Use the sample text pages to answer the questions, and identify where in the reading you found information about the focused question: (page #, paragraph, etc.)
Concept/Question 1:	What is the function of the iris?	
Concept/Question 2:	Why does the pupil constrict or dilate?	

Concept/Question 3:	How large is the lens in someone's eye?	
Concept/Question 4:	Why do the muscles of the lens cause it to change shape?	
Concept/Question 5:	What is accommodation?	
Concept/Question 6:	What is the function of the retina?	

Concept/Question 7:	Describe visual acuity.	
Concept/Question 8:	Another name for nearsightedness is _____?	
Concept/Question 9:	What is farsightedness?	
Concept/Question 10:	How do myopia and hyperopia differ?	

Concept/Question 11:	How does one correct myopia or hyperopia?	
Concept/Question 12:	What is a cataract?	
Concept/Question 13:	At what age range are cataracts common?	
Concept/Question 14:	How is the eye like a camera?	

Concept/Question 15:	How do concave and convex lenses work?	
Concept/Question 16:	True or False: The size of the pupil changes with varying emotions.	

Sample Reading for Module 2

The Eye

From the cornea, light passes through a chamber of fluid called *aqueous humor,* which supplies oxygen and other nutrients to the cornea and lens. Unlike blood, which performs this function in other parts of the body, the aqueous humor is a clear fluid, so light can pass through it. Next, light travels through an opening in the center of the **iris** (the pigmented tissue that gives the eye its blue, green, or brown color); this opening is the pupil. Muscle fibers in the iris cause the pupil to expand (dilate) or constrict to regulate the amount of light entering the eye. The size of the pupil also changes with different psychological states, such as fear, excitement, interest, and sexual arousal. Experienced gamblers (and perhaps Don Juans) can use pupil size to read other people's emotions (Hess, 1965).

The next step in focusing light occurs in the **lens,** an elastic, disc-shaped structure about the size of a lima bean. Muscles attached to cells surrounding the lens alter its shape to focus on objects at various distances. The lens flattens for distant objects and becomes more rounded or spherical for closer objects, a process known as **accommodation.** The light is then projected through the *vitreous humor* (a clear, gelatinous liquid) onto the **retina,** a light-sensitive layer of tissue at the back of the eye. The retina receives a constant flow of images as people turn their heads and eyes or move through space.

The size of the pupils changes in different emotional states, which means that a skilled gambler may literally be able to read his opponents' hands from their eyes, although he may have no awareness of the mechanisms by which he can do this.

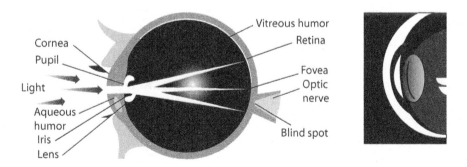

Figure 4.7 Anatomy of the human eye. The cornea, pupil, and lens focus a pattern of light onto the retina, which then transduces the retinal image into neural signals carried to the brain by the optic nerve.

Abnormalities in the eye sometimes make accommodation difficult, affecting **visual acuity,** or sharpness of the image. Since light waves normally spread out over a distance, the eye has to focus them on a single point in the retina to produce a clear image. **Nearsightedness** (or **myopia)** occurs when the cornea and lens focus this image in front of the retina; by the time rays of light reach the retina, they have begun to cross, leading to a blurred image (Figure 4.8). The opposite effect occurs in **farsightedness** (or **hyperopia):** The eye focuses light on a point beyond the retina, leading to decreased acuity at close range. Both abnormalities are common at all ages and usually are readily corrected with lenses that alter the optics of the eye. With advancing age, however, losses in visual acuity become more pronounced (Curcio and Drucker, 1993; Fukada et al., 1990; Matjucha and Katz, 1994). The lens becomes more opaque and loses some of its ability to accommodate, and the diameter of the pupil shrinks so that less light reaches the retina. Cataracts, which are common in older people, occur when the lens becomes so cloudy that the person may become almost blind. As a result of age-related changes, the retina of a normal 65-year-old receives only about one-third as much light as that of a 20-year-old (Kline & Schieber, 1985).

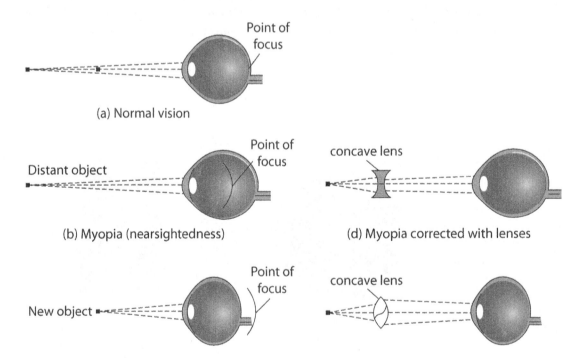

Figure 4.8 Normal vision *(a)*, nearsightedness *(b)*, and farsightedness *(c)*. In *(a)*, the cornea and lens focus the image on the retina, producing normal vision. The shape of the lens, of course, differs for optimal focus on objects nearby or at a distance. In *(b)*, the image is focused in front of the retina (myopia), whereas in *(c)*, it is focused behind the retina (hyperopia). In *(d)*, a concave lens corrects vision by spreading out the light rays from distant objects. In *(e)*, a convex lens has the opposite effect, bending light rays toward each other to focus them on the retina instead of behind it.

Your Text

Try Focused Reading on a chapter from your content area class that you need to read this week.

CHAPTER: **PAGES:**

> Actively bring what you are reading about into the structures of your mind.
> This is both a 'pre-reading' activity and a 'during the reading' activity.

Write the concepts or questions you are focusing on here:

Focused Questions:		Answer to the question, and where in the reading you found information about your focused question: (page #, paragraph, etc.)
Concept/Question 1:		
Concept/Question 2:		
Concept/Question 3:		

Concept/Question 4:		
Concept/Question 5:		
Concept/Question 6:		
Concept/Question 7:		
Concept/Question 8:		
Concept/Question 9:		

Focused Reading can be enhanced when you know the chapter structure and all that is offered within. Complete this **textbook chapter analysis** by previewing a chapter in your textbook and examining the structure. Use the chart to comment on the notable features.

chapter structure: length, section length, notable features	introduction and conclusion	section structure	special features	study aids

strategic plan:

overall reaction:

Strategy Feedback Prompt

This reflection is to be finished after you apply the strategy to your content area textbook. This exercise is meant to be reflective in nature as you consider how you liked the strategy. Finish completing the prompt **after** you apply the strategy to your content area textbook.

> Learning to think about what works for you is important as you take command of your learning.

Module #:
Module Name:

Describe how to do the strategy in detail:

Chapter title and number worked on today:

Outcome: Write a paragraph about your use of the strategy with your own textbook. Comment on the following and add any other thoughts that you would like to share: *How well did the strategy work on your own textbook chapter? Did you have to adjust the strategy when applying it to your own textbook chapter? How? What did you get out of this module?*

Mastery Assessment

The Mastery Assessment for this module involves focusing on questions and reading to find the answers. As you read, fill in the chart.

> You will need to assess your learning in order to discover your strengths and weaknesses.

What goes here?		What goes here?
Concept/Question 1:		
Concept/Question 2:		
Concept/Question 3:		
Concept/Question 4:		

Concept/Question 5:		
Concept/Question 6:		

How does this information that you just read about connect with something else you are learning about?

Identify four Time, Place, and/or Perspective Strategies below:

Module 3

Vocabulary Development

Introduction

There is no quick-and-easy way to increase your vocabulary, although research shows that **reading a lot—of anything—increases your general vocabulary level.** What we are concerned with here, though is **remembering new vocabulary that is specific to your content class.** One of the best ways to do this is to use a system of 3x5 cards as you read.

> Learning new terms is vital to understanding the content of the chapter.

Step-by-Step Strategy Description

1. While reading, when you come across a word you don't know and/or a word that is obviously important to that chapter (it's bolded, underlined, repeated, etc.) **write that word down on the front of a 3x5 index card.**
2. The next step is to figure out what the word means. Read around the word—the previous sentence, the next sentence, etc.—to see if the word is defined in the text. Go to your textbook's glossary and look it up. Finally, if it's not in the glossary, look it up in another dictionary. Then, **write down the definition on the other side of the 3x5 index card.**
3. Next, **write down the sentence you found the word in on the same side of the index card as the definition.**
4. Finally, **figure out how the word is used from the work you've already done with the word, and write your own sentence using the word on the same side of the card as the definition and the other sentence.**

> Illustrating each term is a technique that will help you understand the term.

So the front of the card should look like this:

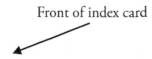

Front of index card

(vocabulary word)

the back of the card should look like this:

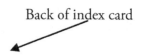

Back of index card

1. *(Definition of vocab word)*
2. *(sentence you found the vocab word in)*
3. *(your own sentence, using the vocabulary word)*

Practice with the example textbook excerpt to be sure you are ready to attempt them on your textbook chapter for homework.

This is a 'during the reading' and an 'after the reading' activity.

Using index cards can help you check your understanding of the text.
Use 3x5 note cards and set them up like this:

FRONT OF CARD   BACK OF CARD

(vocabulary word 1)   1.

                                            2.

                                            3.

(vocabulary word 2)   1.

                                            2.

                                            3.

(vocabulary word 3)

1.

2.

3.

(vocabulary word 4)

1.

2.

3.

Using the sample reading, try this strategy for five vocabulary words.

Sample Reading for Module 3

Classical Conditioning

Classical conditioning (sometimes called *Pavlovian* or *respondent conditioning)* was the first type of learning to be studied systematically In the late nineteenth century the Russian physiologist Ivan Pavlov (1849–1936) was studying the digestive systems of dogs (research for which he won a Nobel Prize). During the course of his work, he noticed a peculiar phenomenon. Like humans and other animals, dogs normally salivate when presented with food, which is a simple reflex. A **reflex** is a behavior that is elicited automatically by an environmental stimulus, such as the knee-jerk reflex elicited by a doctor's rubber hammer. A **stimulus** is something in the environment that elicits a response. Pavlov noticed that if a stimulus, such as a bell or tuning fork ringing, repeatedly occurred just as a dog was about to be fed, the dog would start to salivate when it heard the bell, even if food were not presented. As Pavlov understood it, the dog had learned to associate the bell with food, and because food produced the reflex of salivation, the bell also came to produce the reflex.

Pavlov's Model

An innate reflex such as salivation to food is an unconditioned reflex. **Conditioning** is a form of learning; hence, an **unconditioned reflex** is a reflex that occurs naturally, without any prior learning. The stimulus that produces the response in an unconditioned reflex—in this case, food—is called an **unconditioned stimulus, (UCS).** An unconditioned stimulus activates a reflexive response without any-learning having taken place; thus, the reflex is unlearned, or unconditioned. An **unconditioned response (UCR)** is a response that does not have to be learned. In Pavlov's experiment, the UCR was salivation.

Figure 5.1 Pavlov's dogs. Pavlov's research with dogs documented the phenomenon of classical conditioning. Actually his dogs became conditioned to salivate in response to many aspects of the experimental situation and not just to bells or tuning forks; the sight of the experimenter and the harness, too, could elicit the conditioned response.

Your Text

Try the Index Card Vocabulary Development strategy on a chapter from your content area.

CHAPTER: **PAGES:**

> Tie the new terms into your thinking by connecting them with other important ideas and applying them to your everyday life.

Strategy Feedback Prompt

This exercise is meant to be reflective in nature as you consider how you liked the strategy. Finish completing the prompt **after** you apply the strategy to your content area textbook.

> Learning to think about what works for you is important as you take command of your learning.

Module #:
Module Name:

Describe how to do the strategy in detail:

Chapter title and number worked on today:

Outcome: Write a paragraph about your use of the strategy with your own textbook. Comment on the following and add any other thoughts that you would like to share: *How well did the strategy work on your own textbook chapter? Did you have to adjust the strategy when applying it to your own textbook chapter? How? What did you get out of this module?*

Mastery Assessment

The Mastery Assessment for this module will involve describing the vocabulary index card strategy and practicing it.

> You will need to assess your learning in order to discover your strengths and weaknesses.

Website Resources

Check out a technology strategy to help with learning new terms and concepts:

www.studyblue.com – premade flashcards on a number of topics. App opportunity for iphone, ipad, android, and web use so you can study on the go.

www.studystack.com – premade flashcards on a number of topics. Includes opportunity for matching, hangman, crosswords, quizzes etc.

www.crosswordpuzzlegames.com – make your own crossword puzzle using your own terms.

Find an additional site that would be useful to use for learning new terms and concepts and list it here:

Module 4

Structure Glance

Introduction

This strategy is an important one, and you'll see it reflected in more comprehensive strategies as the strategy work progresses. It is an excellent way to **prepare your mind to comprehend a chapter—using prediction.**

> Pre-reading activities can assist you to successfully read and understand the chapter. You make connections to the reading even before you have done the reading.

In this exercise, you will find three columns. The first column, "*Write The Headings Here*" is simply a **rewriting of the headings used in the chapter.** The second column, "*Write Your Predictions Here*" is a place for you to **record your own thoughts about what each section is probably about.** And in the third column, "*After Reading Each Section: Predictions Right or Wrong?*" **record whether your predictions were right or wrong after reading each section.** If you were more or less right, first check it off, then take any additional notes. If your prediction was off the mark, **record what that section is actually about.** The point of this is not to see if you can guess correctly or not, but to get your mind actively engaged in trying to figure out where the chapter is going.

> Writing down the most basic understanding of a heading is one way to predict what the reading is about.

Step-by-Step Strategy Description

Structure Glance:

1. Read the title and all headings in the chapter once through.
2. Go back to the beginning of the chapter and write the first heading in the first cell of column 1.
3. In the first cell of column 2, write what you think that section will be about, based on the heading.
4. Repeat steps 2 and 3 until you have predicted each section of the chapter.
5. Read the chapter. As you read each section, remind yourself of the heading and what you think will be in that section. After reading each section, pause and decide whether your prediction was right, or if it needs correcting—which will be done in column 3. It is important that the Structure Glance strategy NOT be completed a "column at a time"—that is, by filling out all the headings, then filling out all the predictions, etc. **It needs to be done a heading at a time for it to be useful.** Although it seems unwieldy at first, after a little practice it becomes very fluid.

Write the Headings Here	Write Your Predictions Here (*What you predict each section will be about after reading only the heading*)	Take Notes Here After Reading Each Section: Predictions Right or Wrong? (*If right, check off and take notes. If wrong, record what the section is actually about*).

Using a chart helps you take notes from the text in an organized fashion.

Because you will do this strategy on EVERY heading in a section, knowing how to identify headings is the first step in structure glance. What makes a heading a heading and not just part of the text?

List all the things that make a heading below:

Now look at the following short excerpt with five headings. One way to use Structure Glance is to start thinking about those headings.

What is an Element?

An element is a pure substance that can not be broken down into simpler substances, with different properties, by physical or chemical means. The elements are the basic building blocks of all matter.

Three Types of Elements

Elements can be classified into three types, depending on their properties: metals, nonmetals, and metalloids.

Element Type 1: Metals

Examples of metallic elements are sodium (which has the symbol Na), calcium (Ca), iron (Fe), cobalt (Co), and silver (Ag). These elements are all classified as metals because they have luster, they conduct electricity well, they conduct heat well, and are malleable.

Element Type 2: Nonmetals

Some examples of nonmetals are chlorine, which has the symbol Cl, oxygen (O), carbon (C), and sulfur (S). These elements are classified as nonmetals because they don't shine, they don't conduct electricity well, they don't conduct heat well, and they are not malleable.

Element Type 3: Metalloids

Metalloids have some properties like those of metals and other properties like those of nonmetals. Some examples are arsenic (As), germanium (Ge), and silicon (Si). These particular metalloids are used in manufacturing transistors and other semiconductor devices.

Adapted from Nist & Diehl (2002), pp. 355-6

Write the Headings Here	Write Your Predictions Here *(What you predict each section will be about after reading only the heading)*	Take Notes Here After Reading Each Section: Predictions Right or Wrong? *(If right, check off and take notes. If wrong, record what the section is actually about)*
What is an Element?	*Definition of the term "element"*	√
Three Types of Elements	*Description of the 3 kinds of elements*	*Named the 3 types: metals, nonmetals, metalloids*
Element Type 1: Metals	*define and describe "metals"*	√
Element Type 2: Nonmetals	*define and describe "nonmetals"*	√
Element Type 3: Metalloids	*define and describe "metalloids"*	√

Note that the purpose of Structure Glance is really not to "guess accurately" each of the headings—instead, it is a method of helping you preview the chapter and think about what you will find as you begin reading.

> A prepared mind is more able to absorb the information in the chapter.

Sometimes it is difficult to make a prediction when you know nothing about a particular topic. It is important that you can still make a prediction – use what you know about any of the words to make a prediction. Practice with this heading:

Protein Shapes are Sensitive to the Environment

Think about what you know about protein or shapes or sensitivity or environment. Write your prediction here:

Compare your prediction to those of your classmates.

Think about the reading BEFORE you actually do the reading!

Using the Sample Reading

Try this strategy on the practice textbook excerpt that follows. When you finish, check your work with the text or by comparing your predictions with the predictions of others.

Your prediction, even if inaccurate, will help to understand the issue or topic as you read to see if your prediction is accurate.

Structure Glance Practice

1. Read the title and all headings in the chapter once through. Use the reading on the following pages.
2. Go back to the beginning of the chapter and write the first heading in the first cell of column 1.
3. In the first cell of column 2, write what you think that section will be about, based on the heading.
4. Repeat steps 2 and 3 until you have predicted each section of the chapter.
5. Read the chapter. As you read each section, remind yourself of the heading and what you think will be in that section. After reading each section, pause and decide whether your prediction was right, or if it needs correcting—which will be done in column 3. Take notes in column 3.

Write the Headings Here	Write Your Predictions Here (*What you predict each section will be about after reading only the heading*)	Take Notes Here After Reading Each Section: Predictions Right or Wrong? (*If right, check off and take notes. If wrong, record what the section is actually about*)

Sample Reading for Module 4

INTERIM SUMMARY

During the concrete operational stage, children can mentally manipulate representations of concrete objects in ways that are reversible, as can be seen in their understanding of conservation (that basic properties of an object or situation remain stable even though superficial properties change). The formal operational stage is characterized by the ability to manipulate abstract as well as concrete representations, to reason about formal propositions rather than concrete events. Many of Piaget's broad principles have withstood the test of time, but many specifics of the theory no longer appear accurate.

The Information-Processing Approach to Cognitive Development

The information-processing approach is well suited to sketching some of the finer details of cognitive development. It examines the component processes involved in thinking and focuses on continuous, quantitative changes rather than the broad, qualitative stages studied by Piaget. Information-processing researchers have tried to track down the specific processes that account for cognitive development.

Processing Speed

One of the variables that appears to account most for cognitive development is surprisingly simple: processing speed (Fry & Hale, 1996; Kail, 1991; Miller & Vernon, 1997). As we saw in Chapter 8, mental quickness is a central aspect of intelligence. As children get older, they get faster on a range of cognitive tasks, from categorizing objects to making decisions (Figure 13.12). This allows them, among other things, to hold more information in working memory at any given moment and hence to solve problems more effectively. Speed of processing across a wide array of simple and complex tasks increases throughout childhood and levels off around age 15 (Kail, 1991).

Knowledge Base

Another factor that influences children's cognitive efficiency is accumulated knowledge already in long-term memory, or their knowledge base. Compared to adults, children's knowledge bases are obviously limited because of their comparative inexperience with life (Chi, 1976, 1978). To what extent, then, does the size of children's knowledge base, rather than some other factor, account for their relative cognitive inefficiency?

One study explored this question by reversing the usual state of affairs, selecting children who were *more* knowledgeable than their adult counterparts (Chi, 1978). The cognitive task was to remember arrangements of pieces on a chessboard. Child participants (averaging age 10) were recruited from a local chess tournament, whereas adult participants had no particular skill at chess. The children easily outperformed the adults at remembering the arrangement of pieces on the board, demonstrating that knowledge base was more important than age-related factors in this cognitive task. Other studies have corroborated this finding using stimuli such as cartoon characters with which children are more familiar than adults (Lindberg, 1980).

Automatic Processing

A third factor that influences children's cognitive skill is their increasing ability to perform cognitive tasks automatically (Anderson, 1985; Sternberg, 1984). Automatization refers to the process of executing mental processes with increasing efficiency so that they require less and less attention. In many tasks, from performing addition problems to driving a car, increased competence involves shifting from conscious, controlled processing to automatic, or implicit, processing.

Cognitive Strategies

Children's use of cognitive strategies also develops throughout childhood and adolescence (Siegler, 1996). In memory tasks, young children tend to rely on simple strategies such as rote repetition; older children learn to use increasingly sophisticated, elaborative rehearsal strategies (Chapter 6), such as arranging lists into categories or using imagery (see Alexander & Schwanenflugel, 1994; Brown et al., 1983; Hasselhorn, 1990). In many respects, cognitive development reflects a process akin to evolution: Children try out new "mutations" (different problem-solving strategies), weed out those that do not work as well, and gradually evolve new strategies depending on changes in the situation (Siegler, 1996).

One early study demonstrated differences in the way children of various ages spontaneously use memory strategies (Flavell et al., 1966). The experimenter showed 5-, 7-, and 10-year-old children seven pictures and pointed to three they should remember. Between the time the children saw the pictures and the next phase, when their memory was tested, the experimenter carefully watched them to see whether they used any verbalizations to "think aloud" as an aid to memory. (The researcher was trained at lip reading.) Whereas only 10 percent of the 5-year-olds talked to themselves to help remember the pictures, 60 percent of the 7-year-olds and 85 percent of the 10-year-olds did so.

Metacognition

A final variable involved in cognitive development is **metacognition**—thinking about thinking (Flavell, 1979; Reeve & Brown, 1985; Metcalfe & Shimamura, 1994). To solve problems effectively, people often need to understand how their mind works—how they perform cognitive

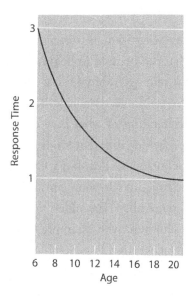

Figure 13.12 Processing speed and age. Here, processing speed (scaled as the ratio of children's speed relative to adult speed) follows an exponential function—and can in fact be predicted with mathematical precision (Kail, 1991). In other words, speed increases rapidly from about ages 6 to 12 and starts to level off by age 15. *Source:* Adapted from Fry & Hale, 1996.

tasks such as remembering, learning, and solving problems. When young children are asked if they understand something, they typically have difficulty discriminating whether they do or not, so they may fail to ask other people or seek information that could inform them (Brown, 1983). Similarly, although preschoolers can recognize under certain circumstances that other people have thoughts or desires (Chapter 14), they do not assume that much is going on in their own and other people's minds when people solve problems, read, write, and so forth (Flavell et al., 1997). For example, they fail to recognize the importance of "inner speech"—using words inside one's head—while performing tasks such as mental arithmetic.

Simply knowing what one does and does not know can be crucial for accurately performing various skills. But how do we know when we really know something or when we are simply guessing or making it up? Knowing something involves a *feeling* of knowing (Conway et al., 1996; Kamas & Reder, 1995). Consider an incident in which a friend and I struggled to recall the name of a famous maker of fine crystal while buying a wedding gift. My friend suggested that the name was something like "Stanford." Somehow "feeling" that she was on the right track, I at first guessed, based, presumably, on my intuitive knowledge of the way memory works, that the name must begin with "St" but then suddenly changed my mind, concluding that the name ended with "-ford." She said it had a British sound to it, I said it had three syllables like "Rutherford," and then she retrieved the *name—Waterford.* Although our exchange may sound more like an example of senile dementia, it illustrates the complex processes involved in knowing what one does and does not know, processes that develop with age.

An important aspect of metacognition is *metamemory*— knowledge about one's own memory and about strategies that can be used to help remember. Metamemory is impaired in many patients with frontal lobe damage (Shimamura, 1995). Not surprisingly, it is also less developed in children, whose frontal lobes remain immature for many years. As they mature, children develop a better understanding of what they can and cannot remember and of the types of strategies useful for approaching different kinds of memory tasks (Flannel & Wellman, 1977; O'Sullivan et al., 1996; Schneider & Pressley, 1989; Yussen & Levy 1975). For example, in one study researchers showed pictures to younger and older children and asked them to predict how many they could remember. The older children's predictions were much more accurate than those of younger children, who often predicted total recall (Fiavell et al., 1970)! Although metamemory, like metacognition in general, often involves explicit processes, many metamemory processes are implicit, such as knowing how, where, and how long to search memory (Reder & Schuss, 1996).

INTERIM SUMMARY: Many aspects of information processing change with age. Among the most important are processing speed, children's knowledge base (store of accumulated knowledge), automatization (executing mental processes automatically and relatively effortlessly, with increasing efficiency and decreased attention), more efficient use of cognitive strategies, and metacognition (knowledge about how one's mind works—or cognition about cognition).

Integrative Theories of Cognitive Development

Piaget's theory views cognitive development as a progression through qualitatively different stages, whereas the information-processing approach focuses on small-scale, quantitative refinements in the child's ability to encode, remember, and process different kinds of information. As different as these viewpoints are, they are not mutually exclusive: Cognitive development may be characterized by both qualitative and quantitative changes and general and specific processes (Fischer, 1980; Fischer & Bideil, 1998).

Theorists who attempt to integrate these views (sometimes called **neo-Piagetian theorists**) agree with several fundamental tenets of Piagetian theory: that children actively structure their understanding, that knowledge progresses from a preconcrete to a concrete and then to an abstract stage, and that all of this occurs in roughly the order and ages reported by Piaget (Bideil & Fischer, 1992; Case, 1992; Fischer, 1980). Like information-processing theorists, however, the neoPiagetians pay more attention to discrete components of cognitive processing than Piaget, and they stress the way cognition develops within specific domains.

Case's Theory

One theory that attempts to wed Piagetian and information-processing models was developed by Robbie Case. Case (1985, 1992, 1998) holds that cognitive development progresses within a general stage framework similar to Piaget's, from a sensorimotor period to an abstract, complex, highly symbolic, formal operational stage. Each stage differs qualitatively from the others in the way children represent problems and strategies for solving them (Case, 1984). Unlike Piaget, Case believes that cognitive progress within each stage is possible because humans are innately motivated to engage in certain types of behaviors, including problem solving, exploration, imitation, and social interaction. Cognitive development occurs within each stage as children set goals, formulate problem-solving strategies, and evaluate the results of those strategies. They then integrate existing problem solving strategies to create more elaborate strategies as new situations arise, and they practice those new strategies until they become automatic.

According to Case, development from one stage to another depends on cultural input, but the factor most responsible for qualitative changes in cognitive development is an increasing capacity for working memory (Chapter 6). Working memory expands with increased automaticity and more efficient use of cognitive strategies, allowing children to keep progressively more things in mind simultaneously and to coordinate previously separate actions and ideas. Attending to both length and width in a conservation task is much easier if a child has large enough working memory capacity to hold both dimensions in mind simultaneously while imagining how, for example, a ball of clay might look if those dimensions changed. Recent research suggests that the central executive function of working memory, which is involved in allocating attention, coordinating different kinds of information held in short-term storage, and handling multiple tasks at once, does in fact continue to develop, at least through age 10 (Hale et al., 1997).

An example of how expanded working memory allows for more complex cognition can be seen in Figure 13.13. In this study, children ages 10 to 18 were asked to draw a picture of a mother looking out the window of her home to see her son playing peek-a-boo with her in the park across the street (Dennis, 1992, cited in Case, 1992). The youngest subjects could not simultaneously coordinate the two scenes. They could keep in mind the image of the mother in the house and the image of the boy in the park, but they could not integrate the two images.

This study illustrates the advantages of Case's neo-Piagetian model over classical Piagetian theory. Certain broad processes, notably limitations in working memory, *constrain* the thinking of the child, providing an upper limit on what a child within a given age range can achieve. This leads to qualitative differences in thought at different stages that appear across a variety of domains (such as art, language, and mathematics), just as Piaget postulated. At the same time, the neoPiagetian model, like similar theories about the way children acquire and coordinate skills (Fischer, 1980), recognizes that development occurs in specific domains and is influenced by culture and experience. By ages 8 to 10, children in Western cultures incorporate artistic conventions developed over the past several centuries for depicting perspective (Chapter 4), such as representing closer objects as larger, but a 4-year-old with a crayon is unlikely to outperform an adult regardless of culture or experience.

An important question that remains is why development follows any broad stages at all, particularly if learning always occurs in specific situations. From North American suburbs to villages in West Africa, children develop basic skills such as counting at approximately the same age, despite wide variations in experience (Case, 1985). Even with extensive practice in counting, young children seem to reach a maximum level of efficiency beyond which they cannot progress at their stage of development (Kurland, 1981). Case proposes a maturational explanation: the myelination of the prefrontal cortex, which plays a central role in working memory and continues to develop through at least early adolescence.

INTERIM SUMMARY: Integrative theories, often called **neo-Piagetian,** attempt to integrate an understanding of the broad stages of Piaget's theory, which suggests progressive ability to coordinate mental representations and think abstractly, with an information processing approach. According to Case's theory, the main variable responsible for cognitive development *across* stages is expansion of working memory capacity.

Cognitive Development and Change In Adulthood

All cultures consider adolescents and adults better decision makers than children, but they differ dramatically in their beliefs about cognition and aging. Many cultures associate age with wisdom. In contrast, Western cultures tend to associate it with decline, although they are ambiguous about when this decline begins and whether middle age confers cognitive advantages over youth. In the United States, for example, people can vote at 18, but the minimum age to run for the presidency is 35. Apparently, the framers of the Constitution held some implicit theory of cognitive development in adulthood, even though most contemporary North Americans believe that some cognitive functions, such as memory, decline by the 40s (see Ryan, 1992).

Figure 13.13 Artistic skill and working memory. Subjects ages 10 to 18 were asked to draw a picture of a mother looking out the window to see her son playing peek-a-boo with her in the park. The 10-year-old who drew this picture accurately depicted both *parts* of the scene but failed to integrate them, drawing the mother and son both facing the artist instead of each other.

Experimental data are similarly ambiguous about cognition in middle age. Many measures of memory show steady declines in adulthood, with young adults performing better than both middle-aged and older adults (Figure 13.14). On other tasks, however, people in their early 20s and 40s perform equally well, and both groups outperform their elders (Lavigne & Finley, 1990).

Your Text

Try this strategy on a chapter from your content area class that you need to read this week. Use the chart on the next page.

CHAPTER: **PAGES:**

> Using a chart to practice your predictions will help to formalize your thoughts. Make connections to the chapter by linking the content to what you already know. Your predictions can be used to check your thoughts with and against the text.

1. Read the title and all headings in the chapter once through - use your content area textbook.
2. Go back to the beginning of the chapter and write the first heading in the first cell of column 1.
3. In the first cell of column 2, write what you think that section will be about, based on the heading.
4. Repeat steps 2 and 3 until you have predicted each section of the chapter.
5. Read the chapter. As you read each section, remind yourself of the heading and what you think will be in that section. After reading each section, pause and decide whether your prediction was right, or if it needs correcting—which will be done in column 3.

Write the Headings Here	Write Your Predictions Here (*What you predict each section will be about after reading only the heading*)	Take Notes Here After Reading Each Section: Predictions Right or Wrong? (*If right, check off and take notes. If wrong, **record what the section is actually about***)

Strategy Feedback Prompt:

This exercise is meant to be reflective in nature as you consider how you liked the strategy. Finish completing the prompt **after** you apply the strategy to your content area textbook. Use this sheet (attach another page if necessary) to record how you put to use study strategies we discuss in class.

> Learning to think about what works for you is important as you take command of your learning.

Module#:

Module Name:

Describe in detail how to do the strategy:

Chapter title and number worked on today:

Outcome: Write a paragraph about your use of the strategy with your own textbook. Comment on the following and add any other thoughts that you would like to share: *How well did the strategy work on your own textbook chapter? Did you have to adjust the strategy when applying it to your own textbook chapter? How? What did you get out of this module?*

Mastery Assessment

> You will need to assess your learning in order to discover your strengths and weaknesses.

The Mastery Assessment for this module will involve more practice in making predictions based on what you already know.

Structure Glance Mastery Assessment

What goes here?	*What goes here?*	What goes here?
1		
2		
3		

4		
5		
6		
7		
8		
9		
10		

Something to Think About

Prediction is a powerful comprehension tool because it helps you connect to the reading before you have even read the reading. If you struggle with this strategy, there are fun ways to practice it.

1.) CARTOONS: Reading cartoons is an excellent way to boost your critical thinking abilities and help you understand how helpful predictions can be. Follow these steps to use Structure Glance with cartoons:

    a) Before reading the words in the cartoon, study the pictures.

    b) Try to guess what the characters are saying by covering up the bubbles and guessing their actual words.

    c) Then check your prediction by reading their words.

2.) GRAPHIC WORDLESS NOVELS: There are several graphic wordless novels that are fun to read. Because these novels have no words, you are building your critical thinking and your prediction skills while having fun. Follow these steps to use Structure Glance with graphic novels:

    a) Study the pictures carefully, page by page.

    b) Think about the message the illustrator conveys with each page.

    c) Imagine what the characters are saying and feeling. Imagine the message.

    d) Guess what the words would be if they were on the page.

    e) Read the entire book page by page as you look for clues to the hidden messages.

Check out wordless graphic novels on the web.

Module 5

HIT: Headings, Ideas, Terms

Introduction

This strategy is a useful way of sorting the chapter so you can begin to identify the main ideas and the significant details within each idea. It is particularly helpful as you complete the chart because you are actually completing a study guide for future use.

> Meaning making from textbooks is like construction: build a foundation of knowledge with the headings and add layers of new information with the content.

In the activity, you will find three columns. The first column, "*Write The Headings Here*" is simply a **rewriting of the headings used in the chapter**. The second column, "Ideas" is a place for you to **record the ideas that you feel are important and you want to try to remember them for future tests**. And in the third column, "Terms" is for you to merely list the terms that you will later make index cards for or use some other strategy for a study guide.

> There is so much information in textbooks that it can be overwhelming. Each heading will have several main ideas.

Step-by-Step Strategy Description:

1. Read the title and all headings in the chapter once through.
2. Go back to the beginning of the chapter and write the first heading in the first cell of column 1.

3. In the first cell of column 2, as you read, write down important things that you want to remember. Try not to copy from the text but put those ideas in your own words to prove that you understand them.

4. Continue to read the chapter. As you are reading each section, make a list of the bolded words that you come across. Do **not** write their definitions here, just make the list for you to work with later.

Write the Headings Here	Write Main Ideas Here as You Read (Put the main ideas in your own words. You will have MANY ideas for each heading.)	As You Read, List the Bolded Terms (do not define them here—you are just making a list of them to study later)

Using a chart helps you take notes from the text in an organized fashion.

Using the sample reading that follows, try this strategy on the practice textbook excerpt. Make a chart like the one following the reading. Please note that many chapters begin with a mini-summary of the previous section. This summarizes the preceding section and leads the reader into the next topic. This reading begins with an interim summary of the previous section. The section title Altruism begins the next reading.

Sample Reading for Module 5

INTERIM SUMMARY: Several factors lead to interpersonal attraction, including proximity, interpersonal rewards, similarity, and physical attractiveness. Psychologists have proposed various taxonomies of love. One contrasts **passionate love** (marked by intense physiological arousal and absorption in another person) with **companionate love** (love that involves deep affection, friendship, and emotional intimacy). Some theorists argue that romantic love is a continuation of infant attachment mechanisms. Evolutionary theorists emphasize **sexual strategies,** tactics used in selecting mates, which vary by gender and reflect the different evolutionary selection pressures on males and females. Love appears to be rooted in attachment but is shaped by culture and experience. The decision to stay in a relationship often involves a balancing act, weighing factors such as its costs and benefits, one's prior investment in it, and the attractiveness of alternatives.

Altruism

Thus far, we have focused on the ties that bind. In this section, we examine another interpersonal process that brings people together: altruism. A person who donates blood, volunteers in a soup kitchen, or risks death (like the heroes of Oliner's World War II odyssey that opened this chapter) is displaying altruism. Some altruistic behavior is so common that we take it for granted—holding open a door, giving a stranger direction, or trying to make someone feel comfortable during a conversation. Indeed, charitable contributions in the United States alone exceed $50 billion a year (Batson, 1995). We begin this section by examining theories of altruism. We then consider experimental research on a particular form of altruism, bystander intervention.

> *Did you never see little dogs caressing and playing with one another, so that you might say there is nothing more friendly? But that you may know what friendship is, throw a bit of flesh among them, and you will learn. Throw between yourself and your son a little estate, then you will know how soon he will wish to bury you and how soon you wish your son to die_____ For universally, be not deceived, every animal is attached to nothing so much as to its own interest_____ For where the I and Mine are placed, to that place of necessity the animal inclines.*
> Epictetus

Theories of Altruism

For centuries, philosophers have debated whether any prosocial act—no matter how generous or unselfish it may appear on the surface—is truly altruistic. When people offer money to a homeless person on the subway, is their action motivated by a pure desire to help, or are they primarily alleviating their own discomfort?

Ethical Hedonism

Many philosophers argue for **ethical hedonism,** the doctrine that all behavior, no matter how apparently altruistic, is—and should be—designed to increase one's own pleasure or reduce one's own pain. As one observer put it, "Scratch an 'altruist' and watch a 'hypocrite' bleed (Gheslin, cited in Batson, 1995).

People have many selfish reasons to behave selflessly (Batson, 1991, 1998). People are frequently motivated by their emotions [...], and behaving altruistically can produce positive emotions and diminish negative ones. The overwhelming majority of Oliner's subjects who saved Jews from the Nazis reported that their emotions—pity, compassion, concern, or affection—drove them to help (Oliner & Oliner, 1988). Prosocial acts can also lead to material and social rewards (gifts, thanks, and the esteem of others) as well as to positive feelings about oneself that come from meeting one's ideal-self standards.

Behaving prosocially can also reduce negative feelings. Some theorists explain the motivation to act on another's behalf in terms of *empathic distress:* Helping relieves the negative feelings aroused through empathy with a person in distress (Hoffman, 1982). This mechanism does not appear to be unique to humans. In one study, researchers trained rhesus monkeys to pull a chain to receive food (Masserman et al., 1964). Once the monkeys learned the response, the investigators placed another monkey in an adjacent cage, who received an electric shock every time they pulled the chain. Despite the reward, the monkeys stopped pulling the chain, even starving themselves for days to avoid causing suffering in the other monkey.

Empathizing with others apparently does involve actually *feeling* some of the things they feel. In one experiment, participants watched videotaped interactions between spouses and were asked to rate the degree of positive or negative affect one of the spouses was feeling at each instant (Levenson & Ruef, 1992). To assess the accuracy of these ratings, the experimenters correlated participants' ratings with the spouses' own ratings of how they felt at each point. Participants who accurately gauged these feelings showed a pattern of physiology similar to the person with whom they were empathizing, such as a similar level of skin conductance (but this was true only for unpleasant emotions). In other words, when people "feel for" another's pain, they do just that—feel something similar, if less intensely—and use this feeling to gauge the other person's feeling. With positive emotions, people apparently use their head instead of their gut.

> *How selfish soever man may be supposed, there are evidently some principles in his nature, which interest him in the fortune of others, and render their happiness necessary to him, though he derives nothing from it except the pleasure of seeing it. Of this kind is pity or compassion, the emotion which we feel for the misery of others, when we either see it, or are made to conceive it in a very lively manner.*
>
> Adam Smith, 1759,
> A Theory of Moral Sentiments

Genuine Altruism

An alternative philosophical position is that people can be genuinely altruistic. Jean-Jacques Rousseau, the French Romantic philosopher, proposed that humans have a natural compassion for one another and that the only reason they do not always behave compassionately is that society beats it out of them. Adam Smith, an early capitalist economist, argued that people are generally self-interested but have a natural empathy for one another that leads them to behave altruistically at times.

Some experimental evidence suggests that Rousseau and Smith may have been right. Empathic people who have the opportunity to escape empathic distress by walking away, or who are offered rewards for doing so, still frequently choose to help someone in distress (Batson, 1991). In addition, people at times behave altruistically for the benefit of a group, usually one with which they identify themselves.

An Evolutionary Perspective

Evolutionary psychologists have taken the debate about altruism a step further be redefining self-interest as reproductive success. By this definition, protecting oneself and one's offspring is in an organism's evolutionary "interest."

Evidence of this type of altruistic behavior abounds in the animal kingdom. Some mother birds will feign a broken wing to draw a predator away from their nest, at considerable potential cost to themselves (Wilson, 1975). Chimpanzees "adopt" orphaned chimps, particularly if they are close relatives (Batson, 1995). If reproductive success is expanded to encompass inclusive fitness [...], one would expect humans and other animals to care preferentially for themselves, their offspring, and their relatives. Organisms that paid little attention to the survival of related others, or animals that indiscriminately invested in kin and nonkin alike, would be less represented in the gene pool with each successive generation. The importance of these evolutionary mechanisms has been documented in humans, who tend to choose to help related others, particularly those who are young (and hence still capable of reproduction), in life and death situations (Burnstein et al., 1994).

Why, then, do people sometimes behave altruistically toward others unrelated to them? Was Mother Teresa an evolutionary anomaly? And why does a flock of black jackdaws swarm to attack a potential predator carrying a black object that resembles a jackdaw, when it means some may be risking their feathers for a bird to which they are genetically unrelated? To answer such questions, evolutionary theorists invoke the concept of **reciprocal altruism,** which holds that natural selection favors animals that behave altruistically if the likely benefit to each individual over time exceeds the likely cost (Caporael & Barron, 1997; Trivers, 1971). In other words, if the dangers are small but the gains in survival and reproduction are large, altruism is an adaptive strategy.

For example, a jackdaw takes a slight risk of injury or death when it screeches or attacks a predator, but its action may save the lives of many other birds in the flock. If most birds in the flock warn one another, they are *all* more likely to survive than if they wander in solitude through the woods like the Transcendentalist philosopher Henry David Thoreau. Thus, altruism can sometimes be more adaptive than "selfishness" (Simon, 1990).

The same argument applies to humans. Social organization for mutual protection, food gathering, and so forth permits far greater reproductive success for each member on the average than a completely individualistic approach that loses the safety of numbers and the advantages of shared knowledge and culture.

Interim Summary: Altruism: refers to behaviors that help other people, with no apparent gain, or with potential cost, to oneself. Philosophers and psychologists disagree as to whether an act can be purely altruistic or whether all apparent altruism is really intended to make the apparent altruist feel better **(ethical hedonism)**. Evolutionary psychologists propose that people act in ways that maximize their inclusive fitness and are more likely to behave altruistically toward relatives than others. Natural selection also favors animals that behave altruistically toward unrelated others if the likely benefit to each individual over time exceeds the likely cost, a phenomenon known as **reciprocal altruism.**

Bystander Intervention

Although philosophers and evolutionists may question the roots of altruism, apparent acts of altruism are so prevalent that their absence can be shocking. A case in point was the brutal 1964 murder of Kitty Genovese in Queens, New York. Arriving home from work at 3:00 a.m., Genovese was attacked over a half-hour period by a knife-wielding assailant. Although her screams and cries brought 38 *of* her neighbors to their windows, not one came to her assistance or even called the police. These bystanders put on their lights, opened their windows, and watched while Genovese was repeatedly stabbed and ultimately murdered.

To understand how a group of law-abiding citizens could fail to help someone who was being murdered, social psychologists John Darley and Bibb Latane (1968) designed several experiments to investigate **bystander intervention,** or helping a stranger in distress. Darley and Latane were particularly interested in whether being part of a group of onlookers affects an individual's sense of responsibility to take action.

In one experiment, male college students arrived for what they thought was an interview (Darley & Latane, 1968). While the students waited to be interviewed, either individually or in groups of three, the investigators pumped smoke into the room through an air vent. Students who were alone reported the smoke 75 percent of the time. In contrast, only 38 percent of the students in groups of three acted, and only 10 percent acted when in the presence of two confederates who behaved as if they were indifferent to the smoke. In another experiment (Latane & Rodin, 1969), college students waited, alone or with one other person, purportedly to participate in a market research study. While waiting, they heard a tape of what sounded like a woman, falling and injuring herself in the next room. Seventy percent of the students who were alone or with a friend tried to help, but only 7 percent of those with a nonresponsive confederate did so.

A Model of Bystander Intervention

Based on these experiments, Darley and Latane developed a multi-stage model of the decision-making process that underlies bystander intervention (Figure 18.5). First, bystanders must notice the emergency. Second, they must interpret the incident as an emergency. Finally, they must assume personal responsibility for intervention. After assuming responsibility, bystanders must then decide how, if at all, they can be helpful, and actually try to help. At any point during these stages, a bystander may make a decision that leads to inaction.

Figure 18.5 Bystander intervention. In the first stage of this decision-making model, the bystander must notice the emergency. In stage two, the bystander must interpret the incident as an emergency. In stage three, the bystander must assume responsibility Once the bystander accepts responsibility, he must then decide what to do and try to do it.

HIT: Headings Ideas Terms

1. Read the title and all headings in the chapter once through.
2. Go back to the beginning of the chapter and write the first heading in column 1.
3. In column 2, as you read, take notes on main ideas you want to remember.
4. As you read the chapter, list the bolded terms in column 3 that you will need to know for your tests.

> This is a 'during the reading' activity. Writing down the most basic main ideas will help you understand the topic under discussion.

Your Text

Try this strategy on a chapter from your content area class that you need to read. On another sheet of paper, identify chapter title, page numbers and then continue by making a **HIT** chart.

CHAPTER: **PAGES:**

Write the Headings Here	Write Main Ideas Here (There are many main ideas for each headed section.)	Write Bolded Terms Here (There are many terms for each headed section.)
Write Heading #1 Here	main idea	1. Term
		2. Term
		3. Term
		4. Term
		5. Term
	main idea	6. ....
	main idea	
	main idea	
	main idea	
	main idea	
	main idea	
Write Heading #2 after you have finished with #1	main idea	
	main idea	
	main idea	
	main idea	

If you do this in your notebook, you can compare your ideas with the professor's lecture.

Strategy Feedback Prompt

This exercise is meant to be reflective in nature as you consider how you liked the strategy. Finish completing the prompt after you apply the strategy to your content area textbook.

> Learning to think about what works for you is important as you take command of your learning.

Module #:
Module Name:

Describe how to do the strategy in detail:

Chapter title and number worked on today:

Outcome: Write a paragraph about your use of the strategy with your own textbook. Comment on the following and add any other thoughts that you would like to share: *How well did the strategy work on your own textbook chapter? Did you have to adjust the strategy when applying it to your own textbook chapter? How? What did you get out of this module?*

Mastery Assessment

> You will need to assess your learning in order to discover your strengths and weaknesses.

The Mastery Assessment for this module involves more practice finding main ideas.
HIT: Headings, Ideas, Terms Mastery Assessment

Answer these questions then make a chart using five headings from your textbook. Fill in the chart as you read.

What goes here?	*What goes here?*	What goes here?

Module 6

NTA: Notes and Text Analysis Lecture Notes vs Textbook Chapter Content

Introduction

The purpose of this strategy is to compare the notes you take in your class with the "notes" of the author of your textbook. As you compare, it is a good idea to fill in ideas and concepts that you may have missed when you were taking notes.

> Note-taking during class will help to create meaning with the text after the class.

Step-by-Step Strategy Description:

Start by choosing a section of notes from your notebook (notes that you took during a lecture). If your instructor hands out notes or power point slide notes you may use them.

List the date and general topic of the pages to be
analyzed:_____

_____

1) **Read and reread** the content of your notes.
2) **Highlight your notes and make marginal notation** on important points.
3) **List the concepts or themes** covered here:_____

_____
_____
_____
_____
_____
_____
_____
_____
_____
_____
_____
_____
_____

4) List the textbook pages that correlate with your notes:_____

_____

_____

5) Now read and reread the correlating textbook pages.

6) Highlight and make marginal notation IN YOUR TEXTBOOK on the correlating important points.

7) Add new information from the textbook to your notes to help with your understanding and memorization.

8) Make up 8 test questions that your professor may ask on a quiz or test based on these notes.

> Reading your textbook BEFORE the lecture will help you ask questions during a lecture.

Possible Test Questions

1.

2.

3.

4.

5.

6.

7.

8.

Cornell System of Note Taking

STEP ONE: Before the lecture

Before you go to class, make a 2 ½ inch column on the left side of your paper. The column you have created is called the "recall" column and will be used after the lecture for organizing and consolidating your thoughts.

RECALL COLUMN ⟶

2 ½ INCH	CLASS
	NOTES
	RECORDED
	HERE

STEP TWO: During the Lecture

As you write:
1.   Listen for main ideas. Do not attempt to write down every word the lecturer says.
2.   Record your information in main idea blocks that resemble paragraphs.
3.   Skip lines between ideas.
4.   Write as legibly as possible.
5.   Use meaningful abbreviations.
6.   Do not use a tape recorder instead of notes.

How to get important Information:
1.   Anticipate
     a.   Read the chapters to be discussed
     b.   Formulate questions from the headings and syllabus
2.   Listen for audio clues
     a.   Repetition
     b.   Change of tone
     c.   "This is important…"
     d.   Enumeration
3.   Visual clues
     a.   Handouts
     b.   Writing on the board

STEP THREE: **After the Lecture**

Reduce your notes for the recall column AS SOON AS POSSIBLE. This means, ideally, the same day. Look over each main idea block and decide on a good summary to be written in the recall column. This clue should describe the main idea without giving away the details. The clue could take the form of a question.

The **Recall Column** is **VERY IMPORTANT**! It allows for spaced review and something called Distributed Practice. This means that you take time to review your notes in small amounts rather than wait to review your notes after you have 20 pages of notes. This improves your capacity to remember the information. Ebbinghaus, a famous psychologist, proved in his experiment on memory that the sooner you review the material, the more likely you are to remember it. In other words, elapsed time causes forgetting. Using the recall column also gives you a way to organize your notes for tests and predict test questions.

Strategy Feedback Prompt:

This exercise is meant to be reflective in nature as you consider how you liked the strategy. Finish completing the prompt after you apply the strategy to your content area textbook.

> Learning to think about what works for you is important as you take command of your learning.

Module #:
Module Name:

Describe how to do the strategy in detail:

Chapter title and number worked on today:

Outcome: Write a paragraph about your use of the strategy with your own textbook. Comment on the following and add any other thoughts that you would like to share: *How well did the strategy work on your own textbook chapter? Did you have to adjust the strategy when applying it to your own textbook chapter? How? What did you get out of this module?*

Mastery Assessment

> You will need to assess your learning in order to discover your strengths and weaknesses.

The Mastery Assessment for this module involves reviewing your notes and answering probable test questions.

NTA: Notes Text Analysis Mastery Assessment
Write out the answers to your eight possible test questions from page 82 here:

1.

2.

3.

4.

5.

6.

7.

8.

Module 7

SQ3R

Introduction

SQ3R was designed by Francis P. Robinson during World War II to help military personnel more effectively read and study. The initials stand for:

S—Survey
Q—Question
R—Read
R—Recite
R—Review

> Reading the chapter in one sitting is a daunting task. It is better to break it down heading by heading.

This is **not a quick-and-easy reading strategy**, and for that reason many students find it takes some patience. But deliberate, thorough application of SQ3R results in rarely having to go back and reread a chapter. In the end, **applying SQ3R well on a chapter is faster than reading it without focus twice.**

Each step of SQ3R must be done in turn, as each step follows up on the step before. The first two steps, "Survey" and "Question" are similar to the first two steps in the "Structure Glance" module.

Step-by-Step Strategy Description:

1. S—Survey: This is a **one or two minute glance** at the title of the chapter, the introductory paragraph (if there is one), all the headings in the chapter, and the summarizing paragraph (if there is one). The purpose is to get a rough idea about what the chapter generally covers and where it's headed.

2. Q—Question: Here's where the work begins. **Next to each heading in the text, create and jot down a question out of the heading** (or, if you can't write in the text for some reason, write out each heading in one column and jot the question down in a corresponding column). For example, if the heading is

<u>Systems for Classifying Subcultures</u>

a possible question could be:

What are the different systems for classifying subcultures?

Using **what, where, when, why, how** questions often works well here. The point is to phrase the question so that you are **reading to find the answer to something**—which leads us to step 3. This is active reading.

3. R—Read: **Read the first section with a focus on answering the question you posed from the section's heading** in step 2. Note that you are not simply moving through the section, but reading for a definite purpose. Read and highlight when you find the answer or other main ideas.

4. R—Recite: This is where you test yourself. **After reading the first section, try to answer your "heading question" without looking at the section**. If you can't answer the question, look back over that section until you can. If you can answer your question well, then you're ready to move onto the next section. Repeat steps 2, 3, and 4 until you've finished the chapter.

5. R—Review: This step is best done both immediately after finishing the chapter and again as a review before a test. **Covering up the section itself, look at each heading and the questions you created, then recite the main points in that section.** Reexamine any section that you aren't able to provide the main points to.

> Incorporating questioning into your strategy work aids memory recall.

THE Q IN SQ3R

The Q in SQ3R is extremely important because it helps with comprehension as your questions will lead you to the main points in each headed section. Studies show that students who read an assignment in order to answer questions based on it, understand the material better—and remember it longer—than do equally capable students who read and reread the same assignment without the aid of questions.

Advantages of questioning before reading:

1.

2.

3.

Sources of questions—what other parts of the chapter, other than the headings, can you question?

1.

2.

3.

4.

5.

6.

7.

How to ask questions:

1. Ask questions **before** not **after** reading. "Before" questions are more helpful for efficient learning than "after" questions.
2. Chapter titles, main headings, and subheadings can easily be turned into questions to help make important points stand out.
3. Unfamiliar terms can suggest questions.
4. Change or add to your original questions as you read in order to encompass all the important ideas.
5. When you ask a question, try to guess the answer to it before you read to find the answer. Retention of learned material is better when learning is connected with some emotional reaction.

Kinds of questions

Surface: who, what, when, where, how.

Depth: encourage a more active thinking process. For example: in what way, compare or contrast, predict, why.

> Questions elicit deep thinking. Write the questions right next to the headings. Don't be afraid to write in your book.

Using the sample reading that follows, try this strategy on the textbook excerpt.

There are six headings in this excerpt. Survey the reading and list them here.

1.

2.

3.

4.

5.

6.

Next to each heading in the text, create and write down a question. Write it in the text right next to the heading. As you read, highlight the answer to your question. If you do not find the answer, highlight what you think is important. Then work through the reading using the remaining steps. Complete one headed section at a time before moving to the next section.

> Writing the questions in your textbook will help you know what to highlight. You can review your questions and your highlighting as you study for tests.

Sample Reading for Module 7

ANXIETY DISORDERS

Anxiety, like sadness, is a normal feeling. Anxiety typically functions as an internal alarm bell that warns of potential danger. In anxiety disorders, however, the individual is subject to false alarms that may be intense, frequent, or even continuous. These false alarms may lead to dysfunctional avoidance behavior, as when a person refuses to leave the house for fear of a panic attack.

Anxiety disorders are the most frequently occurring category of mental disorders in the general population (American Psychiatric Association, 1994). Women are twice as likely as men to be inflicted; this gender difference already edits by age 6 (Lewinsohn et al., 1998). Although many anxiety disorders are triggered under particular circumstances, some people (about 2 percent of the population) have a **generalized anxiety disorder**, characterized by persistent anxiety at a moderate but disturbing level and excessive and unrealistic worry about life circumstances (Rapee, 1991).

Types of Anxiety Disorders

In this section we review the symptoms of some other common anxiety disorders. Although we discuss them separately, people with one anxiety disorder often have others (Barlow et al., 1998; Kindler et al., 1992).

Phobia

At any given time, about 5 percent of the population have at least one irrational fear, or phobia, and more than twice that percent have a phobia at some point in their lifetimes (Magee et al., 1996). For most people, mild phobic responses to spiders or snakes have minimal effect on their lives; for others with diagnosable phobias, irrational fears can be extremely uncomfortable, such as fear of riding in airplanes.

A common type of phobia is social phobia, a marked fear that occurs when the person is in a specific modal or performance situation, such as intense public speaking anxiety. The lifetime prevalence for this disorder is almost 15 percent (Magee et al., 1996). Recent research suggests the potential importance of distinguishing two kinds of social phobias: public speaking phobias, which often occur in people without any other psychiatric problems, and other social phobias, such as intense anxiety at interacting with other people, which typically suggest greater disturbance (Kessler et al., 1998).

Panic Disorder

Panic disorder is characterized by attacks of intense fear and feelings of doom or terror not justified by the situation. The attacks typically include physiological symptoms such as shortness of breath, dizziness, heart palpitations, trembling, and chest pains (Barlow, 1988). Psychological symptoms include fear of dying or going crazy. Lifetime prevalence for panic disorder is in the range of 1.4 to 2.9 percent cross-culturally, in countries as diverse as Canada, New Zealand, and Lebanon (Weissman et al., 1997).

> I was 25 when I had my first attack. It was a few weeks after I'd come home from the hospital. I had had my appendix out. The surgery had gone well, and I wasn't in any danger, which is why I don't understand what happened. But one night I went to sleep and I woke up a few hours later . . . with this vague feeling of apprehension. Mostly I remember how my heart started pounding. And my chest hurt; it felt like someone was standing on my chest. I was so scared, I was sure that I was dying. [Patient cited in Barlow, 1988]

Agoraphobia

A related disorder is **agoraphobia**, a fear of being in places or situations from which escape might be difficult, such as crowded grocery stores or elevators. Between 6 and 7 percent of the population suffer from agoraphobia at some point in their lives (Magee et al., 1996). Agoraphobia can be extremely debilitating; the person may not leave the house because of intense fears of being outside alone, in a crowd, on a bridge, or traveling in a train, car, or bus. Agoraphobia is often instigated by a fear of having a panic attack; ultimately the individual suffering from this disorder may avoid leaving home for fear of having a panic attack in a public place.

Obsessive-Compulsive Disorder

> Mrs. C is a 47-year-old mother of six children who are named in alphabetical order. For 10 years she had been suffering with a compulsion to wash excessively, sometimes 25 to 30 times a day for five to ten-minute intervals. Her daily morning shower lasts two hours, with rituals involving each part of her body . . . If she loses track of her ritual, she must start at the beginning. Mrs. A's compulsions affect her family as well. She does not let family members wear a pair of underwear more than once and prohibits washing them. The family spends large sums of money buying new underwear for daily use. Mrs. A has hoarded various items such as towels, sheets, earrings, and her own clothes for the past two decades. [From Prochaska, 1984]

"I will stop my obsessive-compulsive behavior..."

Try this strategy on the chapter from your content area class.

This module will be practiced **in your text**. You will move through a chapter heading by heading as you follow the steps. Do your **work in your text.**

CHAPTER: **PAGES:**

S   **Survey:** Take a few minutes to **survey** the chapter noting: the title of the chapter, the introductory paragraph (if there is one), all the headings in the chapter, and the summarizing paragraph (if there is one), pictures, charts, graphs, questions, and chapter length. The purpose is to get a rough idea about what the chapter generally covers and where it's headed.

Q   **Question:** Here's where the work begins. **Next to each heading in the text, create and write down a question out of the heading, right next to the heading** (or, if you can't write in the text for some reason, use post it notes).

R   **Read: Read the first section with a focus on answering the question you posed from the section's heading** in step 2. Note that you are not simply moving through the section, but reading for a definite purpose. When you find the answer to the question, **highlight** it. If you do not find the answer, **highlight** other things that you think are important. **READ AND HIGHLIGHT!**

R   **Recite:** This is where you test yourself. **After reading the first section, try to answer your "heading question" without looking at the section.** If you can't recite the answer to the question, look back over that section until you can. If you can answer your question well, then you're ready to move onto the next section.

Repeat step 3, 4, and 5 until you finish the chapter.

R   **Review:** This step is best done both immediately after finishing the chapter and again as a review before a test. **Covering up the section itself, look at each heading, look at each question, and recite the main points in that section.** Reexamine any section that you aren't able to provide the main points.

> Learning to think about what works for you is important as you take command of your learning.

Something to think about: QUESTIONS ABOUT QUESTIONS

Who should ask questions while reading?

The reader should make up questions.

What types of questions can the reader ask?

Who, what, where, when, how questions are surface questions that make it easy to find the answer as you read. In what way, why, compare/contrast, predict are deeper level questions that require more in depth thinking as you read.

Where should the questions be written?

Questions should be written in the margin in complete sentences directly next to the headings or other source used.

When should the reader ask questions?

The reader should ask questions before each headed section is read. The reader can refine the question during the reading process. The reader should make up additional questions after reading. This is a before, during, and after process.

How should the reader ask questions?

The reader should ask questions by turning headings and subheadings into questions. The reader can also use bolded words, tables, charts, graphs, the introduction, conclusion, chapter objectives or anything else found to make up questions.

Why should the reader ask questions?

Questions help improve comprehension. They make it easier to focus on the reading because you have something to look for. They give you a purpose to read so they motivate you to read to find the answer. They also keep you more engaged in the reading process. Any activity that promotes engagement while reading is a good activity to increase comprehension.

Strategy Feedback Prompt

This exercise is meant to be reflective in nature as you consider how you liked the strategy. Finish completing the prompt after you apply the strategy to your content area textbook.

Module #:
Module Name:

Describe how to do the strategy in detail:

Chapter title and number worked on today:

Outcome: Write a paragraph about your use of the strategy with your own textbook. Comment on the following and add any other thoughts that you would like to share: *How well did the strategy work on your own textbook chapter? Did you have to adjust the strategy when applying it to your own textbook chapter? How? What did you get out of this module?*

Mastery Assessment

> You will need to assess your learning in order to discover your strengths and weaknesses.

The Mastery Assessment for this module involves more practice with SQ3R. Practice and show your **work in the text**. You will move through section, by section, heading by heading, as you follow the steps. Do your **work in your text.**

    *Because of the nature of this strategy, your assessment will only include the first 3 steps of SQ3R. It is up to you to recite and review your content course reading as you prepare for tests.

Questions about Questions:

Who should question?

What types of questions can the reader ask?

Where should the questions be written?

When should the reader ask questions?

How should the reader ask questions?

Why should the reader ask questions?

Module 8

Highlighting and Margin Notes

Introduction

The purpose of this module is to **introduce highlighting and note-writing** in the margins of your text as a useful reading/study strategy, and to model, practice, and use this strategy. Underlining can be substituted for highlighting throughout.

Using a variety of strategies prevents boredom when reading.

Highlighting sounds easy—what can be easier than dragging a yellow pen across your textbook, providing firm evidence that you've read the entire chapter? A common approach to highlighting is to highlight so much that by the time a page of highlighting is finished, nearly the whole thing is yellow. Unfortunately, if everything in the chapter is highlighted, going back to look at highlighted parts to review for a test is like re-reading the whole chapter.

So why do some students highlight pretty much the whole page? It probably is partly because they have been told that you highlight the important ideas in a chapter. Well, everything in the chapter is important, or it wouldn't be there! Thus, everything gets highlighted, and highlighting becomes useless as a reading strategy.

There's another way to use the highlighter, though, that doesn't entail highlighting everything in sight. It involves using the highlighter to draw your attention to the **main idea** in each paragraph or section, as well as **important supporting details**—but nothing else. The point is that the highlighter is not there to spell out every little detail, but to remind you of the main idea (and possibly some supporting details) from each section.

Add note-taking in the margins of the text to this method of highlighting. The purpose of margin notes is to add something to what you have highlighted in that section. In fact, **every highlighted section of a page should have a note in the margin that refers to that section**. This usually takes the form of:
- a rewriting of the main idea, if it is already stated in the section
- a formulation of the main idea, if it is not stated in the section and just alluded to

- a note about the purpose of this section; what role it plays within the whole chapter
- your own examples of the point this section makes

Margin notes are useful because they keep you reading actively. Often highlighting turns into a passive activity and needs to be combined with something else to remain useful.

<u>The following paragraph is duplicated to show you different ways of reading academic texts:</u>

- **Method 1: reading without highlighting**

CULTURAL DIFFERENCES OF A NEWBORN CHILD

> Every culture has a quite definite image of what a child is at birth. Russians, for example, see the newborn as so strong that they swaddle it firmly to protect it from harming itself. The French, in contrast, see the baby as fragile and vulnerable to anything harmful in the environment – and they softly swaddle the infant to keep it safe.
>
> In Bali a baby is not given a human name at birth. Until it seems clear it will live, the Balinese refer to it as a caterpillar or a mouse. At three months, when it is given a name, it becomes a participating human being whose mother, speaking for it, says the words of polite social response. But if the baby dies before this, people reproach it, saying" You didn't stay long enough. Next time stay and eat rice with us." For the Balinese believe in reincarnation. They believe the "soul," without any specific personality, is reborn every fourth generation within the same family.   Margaret Mead, "A New Understanding of Childhood"

- **Method 2: reading with highlighting and basic margin notes**   *Main idea*

CULTURAL DIFFERENCES OF A NEWBORN CHILD   *Example #1*

> Every culture has a quite definite image of what a child is at birth. Russians, for example, see the newborn as so strong that they swaddle it firmly to protect it   *Example #2*
> from harming itself. The French, in contrast, see the baby as fragile and vulnerable ———
> to anything harmful in the environment—and they softly swaddle the infant to keep it safe.
>
> In Bali a baby is not given a human name at birth. Until it seems clear it will   *Example #3*
> live, the Balinese refer to it as a caterpillar or a mouse. At three months, when it is
> given a name, it becomes a participating human being whose mother, speaking for
> it, says the words of polite social response. But if the baby dies before this, people
> reproach it, saying "You didn't stay long enough. Next time stay and eat rice with
> us." For the Balinese believe in reincarnation. They believe the "soul," without any
> specific personality, is reborn every fourth generation within the same family.
> Margaret Mead, "A New Understanding of Childhood"

Obviously, the recognizable difference is that one text is marked up and the other is not. Think about the actual reading process. What is the difference in terms of *activity and thought process* that is evident as you review these two paragraphs?

____

____

____

____

Here's another version of what could be highlighted with margin notes that summarize:

- **Method 3: reading with highlighting and rephrased margin notes**

CULTURAL DIFFERENCES OF A NEWBORN CHILD

Every culture has a quite definite image of what a child is at birth. Russians, for example, see the newborn as so strong that they swaddle it firmly to protect it from harming itself. The French, in contrast, see the baby as fragile and vulnerable to anything harmful in the environment—and they softly swaddle the infant to keep it safe.

In Bali a baby is not given a human name at birth. Until it seems clear it will live, the Balinese refer to it as a caterpillar or a mouse. At three months, when it is given a name, it becomes a participating human being whose mother, speaking for it, says the words of polite social response. But if the baby dies before this, people reproach it, saying "You didn't stay long enough. Next time stay and eat rice with us." For the Balinese believe in reincarnation. They believe the "soul," without any specific personality, is reborn every fourth generation within the same family. Margaret Mead, "A New Understanding of Childhood"

Cultures see babies differently.

Russians see strength

French see vulnerability

In *Bali* the baby is a reincarnated family member

Now think about the reading process that is evident. What is the difference in terms of *activity and thought process* using this method? Why would this method be more useful for test preparation?

____

____

____

____

____

____

List the advantages to Method 3:

_____

_____

_____

_____

_____

_____

_____

_____

The only drawback to Method 3 is the amount of time it takes to do this activity. A useful way to think about it is that you are spending time now to save time later. When you read with highlighting AND margin notes, you are actually making study notes for your future tests. If you do it right the first time, you will not have to reread the section at all. Be sure to include everything you want to remember in your margin notes. If you need more room to write, use post-it notes and stick them to the pages.

Step-by-Step Strategy Description:

1. **Preview** the entire chapter you are going to read (by looking at the title and headings, or some other method).
2. You need to highlight and make margin notes **section by section**. Read the first section through quickly, almost skimming, so you get a good idea of what it is about.
3. After skimming the first section, go back to the beginning of the section and **read through at a more normal pace, while stopping to highlight the section's main idea and major supporting details.**
4. **Make notes in the margins** to add something about the main idea, provide an example, point out the purpose of that section, etc.
5. Go on to the next section, and do steps 2-4 for each section until finishing the chapter.
6. A good rule of thumb is that **if you're highlighting more than 20% of each section, you're highlighting too much.**
7. To review the chapter, read the highlighted sections and your margin notes.

> Writing about what you read about will make the reading more meaningful.

Practice highlighting the three brief paragraphs that follow before trying your hand at margin notes.

Paragraph 1:

There are three kinds of book owners. The first has all the standard sets and best-sellers – unread, untouched. (This deluded individual owns wood-pulp and ink, not books.) The second has a great many books – a few of them read through, most of them dipped into, but all of them as clean and shiny as the day they were bought. (This person would probably like to make books his own, but is restrained by a false respect for their physical appearance.) The third has a few books or many – every one of them dip-eared and dilapidated, shaken and loosened by continual use, marked and scribbled in from front to back. (This man owns books.) Mortimer Adler "How to Mark a Book" Saturday Review

Paragraph 2:

The entire body of a tarantula, especially its legs, is thickly clothed with hair. Some of it is short and woolly, some long and stiff. Touching this body hair produces one of two distinct reactions. When the spider is hungry, it responds with an immediate and swift attack. At the touch of a cricket's antennae the tarantula seizes the insect so swiftly that a motion picture taken at the rate of 64 frames per second shows only the result and not the process of capture. But when the spider is not hungry, the stimulation of its hairs merely causes it to shake the touched limb. An insect can walk under its hairy belly unharmed. Alexamder Petrunkevvitch "The Spider and the Wasp"

Paragraph 3:

Physically and psychically women are by far the superior of men. The old chestnut about women being more emotional than men has been forever destroyed by the facts of two great wars. Women under blockade, heavy bombardment, concentration camp confinement, and similar rigors withstand them vastly more successfully than men. The psychiatric casualties of civilian populations under such conditions are mostly masculine and there are far more men in our mental hospitals that there are women. The steady hand at the helm is the hand that has had the practice at rocking the cradle. Because of their greater size and weight, men are physically more powerful than women- - which is not the same thing as saying that they are stronger. A man of the same size and weight as a woman of comparable background and occupational status would probably not be any more powerful than a woman. As far as constitutional strength is concerned, women are stronger than men. Many diseases from which men suffer can be shown to be largely influenced by their relation to the male Y-chromosome. More males die than females. Deaths from almost all causes are more frequent in males of all ages. Though women are more frequently ill than men, they recover from illnesses more easily and more frequently than men. Ashley Montagu, *The Natural Superiority of Women*

Now practice highlighting AND margin notes. Remember, making margin notes is rephrasing the main ideas and writing them in the margin. For every highlighted section, it is important that you also have a margin note summarizing it. This will help you to not only be more selective in what you choose to highlight, but it will also help you process the information and put it in your own words. Try this method on the following paragraphs:

Psychological Effects of Anabolic Steroid Use

There seems to be no question that anabolic steroid use is associated with increased muscle mass and body size, but it is unclear that their use leads to an increase in performance. Stated another way, it may be that increases in performance may be due to the psychological expectancy effect, and only indirectly to anabolic steroid use. This possibility is reinforced by an investigation reported by Maganaris, Collins, and Sharp (2000). Eleven national-level power lifters (bench, dead lift, squat) took two pills immediately before an experimental trial in which they completed a one maximum repetition (1 RM) on all three lifts. The lifters believed that the pills contained an anabolic steroid that would have an immediate action on their strength, when in fact the pills contained saccharin. All 11 lifters improved their lifts above baseline. They were given two more pills for the following week's training. Seven days later, they again completed a second 1 RM lifting trial on all three lifts. Five of the lifters were informed in confidence, just before they made their lifts, that the pills they had been taking contained saccharine. The six lifters who thought they were taking pills containing an anabolic steroid again posted lifts above baseline. The other five lifters did not perform above baseline, and in fact, dropped significantly below baseline. This is the psychological effect.

The long-term effects of anabolic steroid use are unknown. Many sport psychologists believe that long-term use of this drug will lead to poor health. Organs that are particularly susceptible to negative consequence of anabolic steroid abuse are those, such as the kidneys and liver, that are responsible for the transport, metabolism, and detoxification of the drug. Since the liver serves a central role in the metabolism of drugs, it is not surprising that it is frequently damaged by drug use and abuse. If a drug has a negative effect upon even one part of the body, the function of the entire body can suffer (Stone, 1993).

From *Sport Psychology: Concepts and Applications, 6th Edition,* by Richard H. Cox. (468) iRead: The McGraw-Hill Reader

With practice, this strategy takes about as long as simply slowly reading the chapter from start to finish—but you get much more out of it. It helps to think of it as "studying the chapter." When you have finished making your margin notes, you have made a study guide of the chapter! You can then transfer those notes into your notebook or onto study cards or post-it notes. You can also make test questions or an outline of your margin notes. What you do with your margin notes is up to you but they can be a valuable study guide.

Using the sample reading that follows, try this strategy on the textbook excerpt.

Sample Reading from Module 8

INTERIM SUMMARY: Most theorists adopt a diathesis-stress model of schizophrenia. Heritability of schizophrenia is at least 50 percent. According to the **dopamine hypothesis**, positive symptoms of schizophrenia reflect too much dopamine activity in subcortical circuits involving the basal ganglia and limbic system, whereas negative symptoms reflect too little dopamine activity in the prefrontal cortex. Glutamate may also play a role, at least in some individuals with schizophrenia. Other data implicate abnormalities in the structure and function of the brain, such as enlarged **ventricles** and corresponding atrophy (degeneration) in the frontal and temporal lobes. Environmental variables, notably **expressed emotion** (criticism, hostile interchanges, and emotional overinvolvement by family members), play an important role in the onset and course of the disorder. Prenatal and perinatal events that affect the developing nervous system may also be involved in some cases of schizophrenia.

Mood Disorders

Whereas the most striking feature of schizophrenic disorders is disordered thinking, mood disorders are characterized by disturbances in emotion and mood. In most cases the mood disturbance is negative, marked by persistent or severe feelings of sadness and hopelessness, but a mood disturbance can also be dangerously positive, as in manic states. Individuals who are manic feel excessively happy or euphoric and believe they can do anything. As a consequence, they may undertake unrealistic ventures such as starting a new business on a grandiose scale.

Types of Mood Disorders

Depression has been recorded as far back as ancient Egypt, when the condition was called melancholia and treated by priests. Occasional blue periods are a common response to life events such as loss of a job, end of a relationship, or death of a loved one. In a depressive disorder, however, the sadness may emerge without a clear trigger or *precipitant,* continue long after one would reasonably expect, or be far more intense than normal sadness, including intense feelings of worthlessness or even delusions.

Major Depressive Disorder The most severe form of depression is **major depressive disorder**, characterized by depressed mood and loss of interest in pleasurable activities (**anhedonia**). It also includes disturbances in appetite, sleep, energy level, and concentration. People in a major depressive episode may be so fatigued that they sleep day and night or cannot go to work or do household chores because of intense sadness and lethargy. They often feel worthless, shoulder excessive guilt, and are preoccupied with thoughts of suicide. Major depressive episodes typically last about five months (Solomon et al., 1997).

At any given moment, 2 to 3 percent of males and 5 to 9 percent of females suffer from major depression. The lifetime risk for major depressive disorder is 5 to 12 percent in men and 10 to 26 percent in women (APA, 1994). Major depression is a progressive disorder, with episodes gradually increasing in severity. Roughly 75 percent of patients who experience a major depressive episode will have a recurrence within five years (Maj et al., 1992).

Dysthymic Disorder A less severe type of depression is dysthymic disorder. **Dysthymic disorder** (or **dysthymia**) refers to a chronic low-level depression lasting more than 2 years, with intervals of normal moods that never last more than few weeks or months. Dysthymic disorder may include symptoms found in MAJ depression (such as disturbances in sleep, energy, and self-esteem), but they are not debilitating. The effects of dysthymic disorder on functioning are more such as when people who are chronically depressed choose professions that underuse their talents because of a lack of confidence, self-esteem, or motivation.

Bipolar Disorder A manic episode, or **mania,** is characterized by a period abnormally elevated or expansive mood. While manic, a person usually has an inflated sense of self that reaches grandiose proportions. During a manic episode people generally require less sleep, experience their thoughts as racing, and feel constant need to talk. Individuals with **bipolar disorder** have manic episodes and often experience both emotional "poles," depression and mania (in contrast with **unipolar depression,** which involves only depression). About 15 to 20 percent patients who have manic episodes also develop psychotic delusions and hallucinations (Lehmann, 1985).

The lifetime risk for bipolar disorder in the general population is low—some where between 0.5 and 1.6 percent—but it can be one of the most debilitating an lethal psychiatric disorders, with a suicide rate between 10 and 20 percent (Good win & Ghaemi, 1998; MacKinnon et al., 1997). Less severe variants of the disorder in which the individual experiences *hypomanic* episodes (with similar features except less intense), make disorders on the bipolar "spectrum" more common. As we saw [...] patients with cyclothymia, or *cyclothymic disorder,* have in tense mood fluctuations but do not develop full-blown mania. Bipolar disorder appears to occur more frequently in the upper social classes. People with bipolar disorder and their relatives tend to achieve higher levels of education and are disproportionately represented among creative writers and other professional [...].

INTERIM SUMMARY Mood disorders are characterized by disturbances in emotion an mood, including both depressed and **manic** states (characterized by symptoms such as at normally elevated mood, grandiosity, and racing thoughts). The most severe form of depression is **major depressive disorder,** characterized by depressed mood and loss of interest in pleasurable activities. **Dysthymic disorder** refers to a chronic low-level depression lasting more than two years, with intervals of normal moods that never last more than few weeks or months. In **bipolar disorder**, individuals have manic episodes and may also experience intense depression.

Theories of Depression

Depression can arise for many different reasons. As in schizophrenia, biological and psychological processes often interact, with environmental events frequently triggering a biologically based vulnerability. However, unlike schizophrenia, depression is common even among people without a genetic vulnerability.

Genetics Heredity clearly plays a major role in some cases of depression particularly severe forms of major depression, although heritability is considerably lower than in schizophrenia (Lyons et al., 1998; McGuffin et al., 1996; Kendle et al., 1992). Estimated heritabilities for

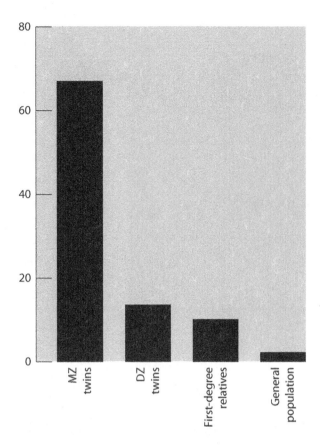

Figure 15.7 Genetics of bipolar disorder. Monozygotic twins have a highly elevated con-cordance rate for bipolar disorder relative to dizygotic twins and other relatives, suggest-ing substantial heritability. *Source:* **Primarily based on D.R MacKinnon, K.R. Jamison, and J.R. DeDavlo (1997). Genetics of manic depressive illness.** *Annual Review of Neuroscience, 20,* **355-373.**

major depression range from about .30 t(.50; for dysthymia they are lower. A family history of depression doubles or triples an individual's risk of a mood disorder. An estimated 50 percent of individuals with unipolar depression have a family history of depression (Winokure al, 1978).

> As you write your margin notes make connections between what you already know and the content in the text. Your connections will help you remember it better.

Your Text

Try this strategy on a chapter from your content area class.

CHAPTER: **PAGES:**

> As you practice this strategy, think about the information. Highlight and write your margin notes section by section before moving on to new information.

Strategy Feedback Prompt

This exercise is meant to be reflective in nature as you consider how you liked the strategy. Finish completing the prompt **after** you apply the strategy to your content area textbook.

Module #:
Module Name:

Describe how to do the strategy in detail

Chapter title and number worked on today:

Outcome: Write a paragraph about your use of the strategy with your own textbook. Comment on the following and add any other thoughts that you would like to share: *How well did the strategy work on your own textbook chapter? Did you have to adjust the strategy when applying it to your own textbook chapter? How? What did you get out of this module?*

Mastery Assessment

The Mastery Assessment for this module involves reading, highlighting, and writing margin notes on a text selection.

You will need to assess your learning in order to discover your strengths and weaknesses.

Module 9

Text Web Connection

Introduction

The purpose of this module is to promote your use of other resources that may help you understand your text. As you know, there are many other ways to retrieve information besides using your textbook and the web is a perfect source. It is important, however, that you retrieve information from credible sources on the web. The best way to find a credible source is to look through your textbook for suggested links. Many textbooks provide links that will include chapter summaries, outlines of chapters, practice test questions, and authentic tests with answer keys so that you can check your comprehension of a chapter. These sources are excellent ways to see what is important in a chapter and to know what to study.

> All forms of media are very engaging and can be useful tools for developing comprehension.

Step-by-Step Strategy Description

> Choosing the correct website to help you requires higher order thinking as you evaluate the various sites.

1. **Preview** your book to see if there are any web addresses in the front of the book.
   (There may be a separate online component to the textbook as well).
2. **Preview** the entire chapter you are going to read to see if any web addresses are listed in the chapter.
3. If you can't find a link in the book, feel free to do an internet search using the chapter or heading title.
4. **Read and review** the material that you find.

5. **Compare** the material to what is in the text. (especially is you are using a resource that isn't provided by the text)
6. **Make** a study guide from the web page **or** use the practice quizzes that are provided.
7. **Print** and hand in your proof of completion.

Using the sample reading that follow, note the different types of resources you may find in a textbook.

The following textbook excerpt is an example to help you know other resources to use.

For Students

Sample Reading for Module 9

Art Notebook: Packaged with every text, this notebook contains all of the art illustrations in *Psychology: Mind, Brain, & Culture* that students will see in lecture from the art slides and transparencies. Students can easily take notes in class on the illustrations contained in the slide shows on the *Instructor's Resource CD-ROM* without having to bring their text to class, and then use this notebook to study for exams.

The Psychology Web Site for Students: Packaged with every text will be a password that will be the students' key to the new Web site. Here students will have access to the latest research through *Science News* articles, updated biweekly and specifically tied into each of the chapters they study. Over 100 Web sites with descriptions researched and written by Paul Wellman will be included on the site, separated by text chapter, that will guide students through the most useful and accurate information available on the Web. Students can take practice quizzes here, written by Professor Runi Mukerji, that are scored and also can be sent directly to their instructors.

Study Guide: Written by Alastair Younger at the University of Ottawa, and edited and reviewed by *The Princeton Review* so it ties in well with the *Test Bank* and *Instructor's Manual,* the study guide offers students a great way to review the material in the text and test their knowledge. Each chapter in the text has a corresponding chapter in the study guide. Six tools help students master the material: chapter outlines, learning objectives, key terms, fill-in exercises, critical thinking exercises, and sample test questions with answers.

On-line Guide: This paperback Web guide will be included with every copy of the text and covers the basics of student use of the Internet and how to use search engines most efficiently to find the exact information you're looking for. A special chapter covering *Mental Health Net* is included as well a complete section of URLs relating Web links to topics in each chapter of the text.

Videos: There are a number of videotapes available to adopters of the text that are new to this edition. Please contact your local Wiley representative for details of this exciting new program.

> Using websites along with your textbook helps you prepare for class.

Your Text

Try this strategy on a chapter from your content area class that you need to read this week. Use the recommended sites from your textbook or search for a reliable site using specific content related search words.

CHAPTER: **PAGES:**

> Be selective when choosing your websites. It is important that it correlates well with the information in your chapter.

Examine the headings in one of your chapters, and use the headings to search the web.

List the web address you will use for this exercise:

_____

_____

_____

_____

Read both the chapter and the site that you chose. Compare and/or contrast this information with the contents of your textbook. List similarities of information here.

_____

_____

_____

_____

_____

_____

_____

Use the additional resource to create a study guide, practice test, or set of notes.
Print your work as evidence of completion. Explain how you used your additional resource.

_____

_____

_____

_____

> Learning to think about what works for you is important as you take command of your learning. Assessing your learning helps you discover your strengths and weaknesses.

Strategy Feedback Prompt:

This exercise is meant to be reflective in nature as you consider how you liked the strategy. Finish completing the prompt **after** you apply the strategy to your content area textbook.

Module #:
Module Name:

Describe how to do the strategy in detail:

Chapter title and number worked on today:

Outcome: Write a paragraph about your use of the strategy with your own textbook. Comment on the following and add any other thoughts that you would like to share: *How well did the strategy work on your own textbook chapter? Did you have to adjust the strategy when applying it to your own textbook chapter? How? What did you get out of this module?*

Mastery Assessment

Based on the information found on the website, take the quiz provided and/or make up your own quiz from the website.

Module 10

CPG: Charts, Pictures, Graphs

Introduction

The purpose of this module is to encourage you to read and understand the charts, pictures, and graphs contained within the chapters of your textbook. For some readers, the charts, pictures, and graphs are skimmed over or not read at all. There is so much text to read and some readers concentrate on the text and never take the time to read the graphics. Yet, the graphics contained within a chapter are there to HELP you understand the text. Many textbooks provide these graphics so that the information is presented in a clear, condensed, visually interesting way. These pictures, charts, and graphs are excellent ways to see what is in the chapter, what is important in a chapter, and what to study.

> Reading charts, pictures, and graphs is another way of applying the content in the chapter.

Step-by-Step Strategy Description

1. Choose a chapter for focus.
2. Identify all the charts, pictures, and graphs.
3. Make 3 columns on your paper. In the first column, list the page number of the chart, picture or graph. In the second column, list the text title or description of the chart, picture, or graph. In the third column, describe in your own words the chart, picture, or graph. For any chart, picture, or graph that you do not understand, find information explaining it within the text.

> Reviewing the examples provided in the text helps solidify the ideas in the chapter.

Using the sample reading that follows, try this strategy on the textbook excerpt.

> Summarizing the information presented in the pictures, charts, and graphs is a good way of knowing the most important points in the reading.

Sample Reading for Module 10

Everyone has had the experience of trying to pay attention to too many things at once-and consequently not understanding or competently performing any of them. Psychologists have tried to determine the extent to which whether people can split attention between two complex tasks, such as following two conversations simultaneously; this is known as **divided attention** (see Craik et al, 1996). One way researchers study divided attention is through **dichotic listening** tasks (Figure 9.1): Subjects are fitted with earphones, and different information is directed into each ear simultaneously. They are instructed to attend only to the information from one ear by repeating aloud what they hear in that ear for a period of time, a process called *shadowing*. Attending to one channel or the other is difficult at first; it is easier if the two channels differ in topic, voice pitch, and so forth (Hirst, 1986).

Subjects can become so adept at shadowing that they are completely unable to recognize information in the unattended channel, performing no better than chance when asked whether a word presented in the unattended channel had been presented. Nevertheless, the information does appear to be processed to some degree, much as the smell of smoke is processed while reading a newspaper. This has been clearly demonstrated in research on priming [...], the process by which exposure to a stimulus (such as a word) affects performance on tasks involving related stimuli (Nisbett & Wilson, 1977; Schacter, 1992). For example, a subject who hears "England" in the unattended channel may have no recollection of having heard the name of any country. When compared to a control subject who has not been similarly primed, however, the individual is more likely to say "London" if asked to name a capital city, and he will more quickly fill in the missing letters when asked for the name of a city when presented with

LO _ _ _ N.

The data from many dichotic listening studies of divided attention actually suggest that subjects may not be dividing their attention at all: Failing to show recognition memory for the prime suggests that participants never consciously attended to it. In other cases, however, people do appear to divide their attention, performing two complex tasks simultaneously. Listening to a lecture while taking notes requires a student to hear and process one idea while simultaneously writing, and even paraphrasing, a previous idea or sentence. This is remarkable because both tasks are verbal and the content of each is highly similar; hence, one would expect heavy interference between the two. Psychologists have even trained subjects to take dictation while reading (Spelkeet al., 1976).

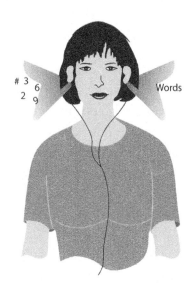

Figure 9.1 A dichotic listening task. Subjects are fitted with earphones, and different information is transmitted into each ear simultaneously. Subjects often show awareness of information in the unattended channel, even when they have no conscious recognition of it.

Sometimes people accomplish such feats by rapidly shifting attention back and forth between the two tasks. Much of the time, however, people solve attentional dilemmas by automatizing one task or the other [...]. Automatization develops through practice, as actions previously performed with deliberate conscious effort are eventually processed automatically. While students listen to a lecture, their primary focus of consciousness is on the lecturer's current words, while a largely automatic process, perhaps drawing on some subset of attentional processes, allows note taking. Precisely how much consciousness is involved in divided attention is not well understood. Students can generally recount what they have just written even while listening to a lecture, suggesting *some* involvement of conscious attention, although their primary allocation of attentional resources is to the lecturer.

INTERIM SUMMARY: Attention refers to the process of focusing conscious awareness, providing heightened sensitivity to a limited range of experience requiring more extensive information processing. Attention consists of at least three functions: orienting to sensory stimuli, controlling the contents of consciousness and voluntary behavior, and maintaining alertness. **Divided attention**, which often involves automatizing one or more tasks or rapidly shifting attention between them, refers to the capacity to split attention or cognitive resources between two or more tasks.

The Normal Flow of Consciousness

A major component of the normal flow of consciousness is **daydreaming**—turning attention away from external stimuli to internal thoughts and imagined scenarios. Some daydreams are pleasurable fantasies, whereas others involve planning for future actions, particularly involving people in important relationships. In one large-scale study of daydreaming, all subjects reported daydreaming daily (Singer, 1975). Another research team found that college students daydream about half the time they are conscious, if daydreaming includes thoughts about something other than what is currently happening in the person's environment, such as thinking about a paper that needs to be written while watching a basketball game or engaging in a less than captivating conversation (Klinger, 1992).

Psychologists study the normal flow of consciousness through **experience-sampling** techniques (Larsen, 1997; Singer & Kolligian, 1987; Wong & Csikszentmihalyi, 1991). In one design, subjects talk aloud, sometimes while performing a task, simply reporting the contents of their consciousness. Psychologists then code their verbal responses into categories, such as emotional tone, relevance to the task at hand, or content.

Beeper Studies

An experience-sampling technique that has provided a more natural window to the flow of consciousness in everyday life is used in beeper studies, in which participants carry pagers and report their experience when "beeped" at various points during the day. In one study, researchers sampled the experience of 75 adolescents from a Chicago high school (Csikszentmihalyi & Larson, 1984). They randomly selected students within each of several categories, including sex, grade, and social class (a stratified random sample; [...]). For one week, participants were beeped at some point during every two-hour period (except, of course, at night), at which time they filled out a brief form reporting what they were doing and with whom, what they were thinking and feeling, and how intensely they were feeling it.

Some of the results were quite unexpected. When subjects were with their families, their negative thoughts outnumbered their positive thoughts by about 10 to 1. When they were asked, "As you were beeped, what were you thinking about?" their responses included "my aunt talks too much" or "how incompetent my mom is" (p. 139). Using this method, the investigators were also able to explore the subjective experience of individual subjects (Figure 9.2).

Culture and Consciousness

We are accustomed to thinking of consciousness as a realm of experience that is uniquely private, but consciousness is in part culturally constructed. Cultural practices and beliefs shape the way people organize their subjective world, including the way they conceive of time and space (Hallowell, 1955; Shore, 1996). In most preindustrial cultures, consciousness is organized into broad units of time, such as sunup and sundown, rather than into the tiny units of time that organize consciousness in cultures ruled by the clock.

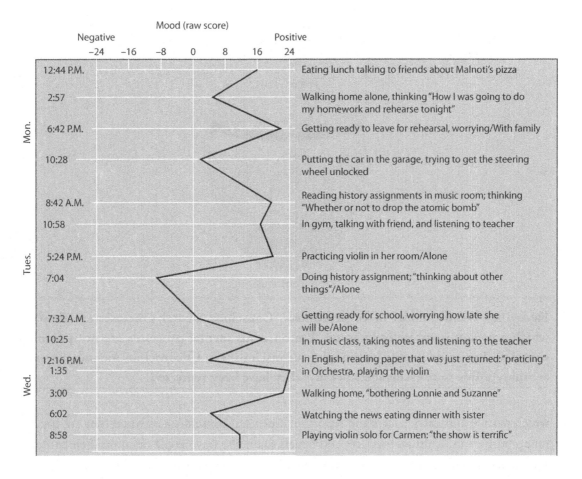

Mood (raw score)

Negative						Positive
−24	−16	−8	0	8	16	24

Mon.

12:44 P.M. — Eating lunch talking to friends about Malnoti's pizza

2:57 — Walking home alone, thinking "How I was going to do my homework and rehearse tonight"

6:42 P.M. — Getting ready to leave for rehearsal, worrying/With family

10:28 — Putting the car in the garage, trying to get the steering wheel unlocked

Tues.

8:42 A.M. — Reading history assignments in music room; thinking "Whether or not to drop the atomic bomb"

10:58 — In gym, talking with friend, and listening to teacher

5:24 P.M. — Practicing violin in her room/Alone

7:04 — Doing history assignment; "thinking about other things"/Alone

Wed.

7:32 A.M. — Getting ready for school, worrying how late she will be/Alone

10:25 — In music class, taking notes and listening to the teacher

12:16 P.M. — In English, reading paper that was just returned: "praticing"
1:35 — in Orchestra, playing the violin

3:00 — Walking home, "bothering Lonnie and Suzanne"

6:02 — Watching the news eating dinner with sister

8:58 — Playing violin solo for Carmen: "the show is terrific"

Figure 9.2 Three days in the life of Katherine. In this experience-sampling study, Katherine reported what she was doing and thinking about whenever she was paged by a beeper. *Source:* **Csikszentmihalyi & Larson, 1984, p. 117.**

Cultural processes also shape the phenomena to which people turn their attention. People in the industrialized West are constantly making inferences about other people's mental states, listening carefully to their words and actions to try to figure out, for example, whether they are sincere—that is, whether they really *mean* what they are saying. In contrast, the Ifaluk of Micronesia, like many preindustrialized peoples, are not so concerned with the inner meanings of social actions (Lutz, 1992). Their moral code revolves around harmony within the group, which is essential for people who must live together on a small island. When people are behaving in ways that maintain this harmony, no one is concerned about whether or not they mean it, since the Ifaluk assume that people behave morally because that is the right thing to do. Further, the kind of introspection valued in many segments of contemporary Western culture, which involves self-reflection, for the purpose of self-knowledge, is not encouraged by Ifaluk values and practices. In fact, the Ifaluk perceive it as a sign of self-absorption (Lutz, 1992).

INTERIM SUMMARY Prominent in the normal flow of conscious experience are **day** dreams, in which the person turns attention away from external stimuli to internal thoughts and imagined scenarios, often for pleasure or for problem solving. Psychologists learn about the normal flow of consciousness through **experience-sampling** techniques, such as beeper studies, in

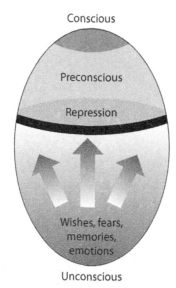

Figure 9.3 Freud's model of consciousness. Conscious mental processes are those of which a person is subjectively aware. Preconscious mental processes are not presently conscious but could readily be brought to consciousness. Unconscious mental processes are inaccessible to consciousness because they have been repressed.

which participants carry pagers and report on aspects of consciousness when they are paged at random intervals. Cultural practices and beliefs shape the way people organize their conscious experience, including the way they conceive of time and space and the extent to which they focus on their own and others' internal states.

Perspectives on Consciousness

Consciousness occupied a central role in the first textbook on psychology, written by William James in 1890, and figured prominently in the work of Freud, who expanded the focus of psychology to include unconscious processes as well. When behaviorism came into ascendance, consciousness as a focus of investigation receded from the consciousness of the scientific community and remained that way until the 1980s. Behaviorists wanted to avoid explaining behaviors in terms of mental events that cannot be observed scientifically, since people's introspective reports are impossible to verify. Behaviorists also rejected the idea of a conscious mind as an agent that chooses, intends, or makes decisions (Skinner, 1974, p. 169). Organisms as primitive as snails respond to environmental contingencies, yet no one would propose that snails therefore have consciousness. Further, according to Skinner, to explain a person's action on the basis of an unconscious process is simply to admit that we have not yet observed the environmental stimuli controlling the behavior.

Until about a decade ago, cognitive psychologists paid little attention to consciousness, either. But as we saw [...] that all changed with the surge of research on implicit memory and cognition. In the last decade, spurred by developments in neuroscience and neuro-imaging that provide a new window *on* consciousness, cognitive scientists—as well as philosophers, neurologists, biologists, and even physicists—have begun rethinking consciousness (e.g., Edelman, 1989; Cohen & Schooler, 1997). In this section we examine psychodynamic and cognitive perspectives on consciousness and explore ways they converge. We then consider what can be learned about normal consciousness by observing neuropsychological patients like Claparede's, who manifest dissociation between what they know consciously and unconsciously.

The Psychodynamic Unconscious

Freud (1900) defined consciousness as one of three mental systems called the conscious, preconscious, and unconscious (Figure 9.3) **Conscious** mental processes are those of which a person is subjectively aware (such as the sentence you just read—if you were paying attention!). **Preconscious** mental processes are not presently conscious but could be readily brought to consciousness if the need arose, such as the smell of bacon cooking in the background or the name of a city that is not currently in mind but could easily be retrieved. **Unconscious processes** are inaccessible to consciousness because they would be too anxiety provoking to acknowledge; that is, they are repressed.

Freud likened repression to a censor. Just as a repressive government censors ideas or wishes it considers threatening, so, too, does the mind censor threatening thoughts from consciousness (Figure 9.3). Thus, a person may remember an abusive father with love and admiration and have little access to unhappy memories because admitting the truth would be painful. Unconscious processes of this sort are *dynamically unconscious*—that is, kept unconscious for a reason, requiring psychological effort or energy (dynamic force) to keep them out of awareness. Freud (1915) recognized that many other psychological processes are *descriptively unconscious*—that is, not conscious even though they are not threatening, such as the processes by which depletion of glucose levels in the blood lead to hunger.

Subliminal Perception

In the 1940s and 1950s, as part of the new look in perception [...], researchers tested hypotheses derived from Freud's theory of consciousness. Studies of **subliminal perception**-the perception of stimuli below the threshold of consciousness—used a device called *a tachistoscope* to flash images, too quickly for conscious recognition but slowly enough to be registered outside awareness (Dixon, 1971, 1981; Erdelyi, 1985; Weinberger, in press). For example, in one study the experimenter flashed one of two pictures subliminally (Figure 9.4). The first depicted a boy behaving aggressively toward a man; the second depicted the boy presenting a man with a birthday cake. Participants were then shown a neutral picture of the boy and asked to judge the boy's personality. Participants exposed to the aggressive picture tended to judge the boy negatively, whereas those who had been flashed the altruistic picture rated him positively.

This line of research drew considerable fire, in part because of methodological concerns, but also in part because the field was still dominated by behaviorism and was not yet ready

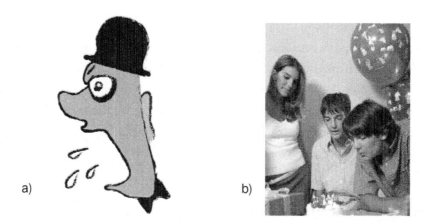

Figure 9.4 Subliminal perception. Participants were presented subliminally with either slide A, a boy behaving aggressively, or B, a boy behaving altruistically. Participants were then shown a neutral picture of the boy and asked to judge his personality. Participants who had seen slide A described the boy as aggressive, whereas those who had seen slide B described him as altruistic.

for the concept of unconscious processes. In recent years, however, both psychodynamic and cognitive researchers have breathed new life into subliminal research, demonstrating that subliminal presentation of stimuli can indeed influence thought and emotion (Bowers, 1984; Neidenthal & Cantor, 1986; Shevrin et al., 1996; Weinberger & Hardaway, 1990). For instance, subliminal presentation of a happy or sad face directly prior to exposure to a novel visual stimulus (such as a Chinese letter) affects the extent to which subjects like it (Murphy

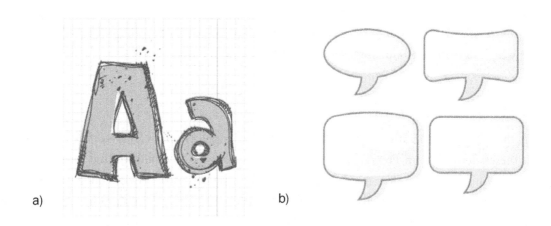

Figure 9.5 Subliminal priming. Participants were presented with either a word or a blank field *(a)*. This stimulus was followed by a mask, a stimulus that would prevent the word or blank field from lingering as a visual memory *(b)*. Participants were then asked to indicate whether a word or a blank had been flashed. Results showed that subliminally presented stimuli can influence thought.

& Zajonc, 1993). Subliminal presentations of the face seems to "tag" the stimulus with an emotional connotation.

In one study, the investigator subliminally presented participants with either a word or blank field (Marcel, 1983). The stimulus was followed immediately by a masking stimulus to prevent it from lingering as a visual memory (Figure 9.5)

Page number of chart, picture, or graph	Title of chart, picure, or graph	Describe in your own words the chart, picture, or graph. For any chart, picture, or graph that you do not understand, find information explaining it within the text.
1		
2		
3		
4		
5		
6		

Your Text

Try this strategy on a chapter from your textbook.

CHAPTER: **PAGES:**

Page number of chart, picture, or graph	*Title of chart, picure, or graph*	*Describe in your own words the chart, picture, or graph. For any chart, picture, or graph that you do not understand, find information explaining it within the text.*
1		
2		
3		
4		
5		
6		

Strategy Feedback Prompt

This exercise is meant to be reflective in nature as you consider how you liked the strategy. Finish completing the prompt after you apply the strategy to your content area textbook.

> Learning to think about what works for you is important as you take command of your learning.

Module #:
Module Name:

Describe how to do the strategy in detail:

Chapter title and number worked on today:

Outcome: Write a paragraph about your use of the strategy with your own textbook. Comment on the following and add any other thoughts that you would like to share: *How well did the strategy work on your own textbook chapter? Did you have to adjust the strategy when applying it to your own textbook chapter? How? What did you get out of this module?*

Mastery Assessment

The Mastery Assessment for this module involves **making up and answering your probable test questions** based on your charts, pictures, and graphs assignment.

> You will need to assess your learning in order to discover your strengths and weaknesses.

CPG: Charts, Pictures, Graphs

Make up probable test questions based on your text assignment and answer these questions.

1.

2.

3.

4.

5.

6.

7.

8.

Module 11

Outlining

Introduction

The purpose of this module is to introduce outlining as a reading and study tool, and to model, practice, and use outlining as a textbook reading strategy.

> Making an outline of the text is a "during – reading" activity.

If your experiences in high school were like many students', you may remember outlining as a tool your English teacher showed you to use as an organizer before writing a paper. Although we are using it a different way here—instead of a pre-writing exercise, it is a reading strategy—it still accomplishes a similar purpose: it helps you organize and remember the text.

There are a couple steps to outlining to be aware of. It would be a mistake to simply read the chapter, and then pick up a pencil to start outlining. The **outlining process begins as you read, and just becomes formalized on another sheet of paper after you read**. By working through the whole process, step-by-step, you will end up with a thorough reading and good study guide to use later.

> Outlining promotes understanding. Adding examples to the outline helps to solidify the ideas in an organized way and aids in memory recall.

Step-by-Step Strategy Description

Directions for Outlining:

1. This part of the process takes place while you read, and involves making notations in the margins of your book.
   a. As you are reading, you need to stay aware of the main idea. If the main idea is fairly well spelled out in the text itself, underline or highlight it, and make

the notation "MI" (main idea) in the margin next to the underlining. Alternatively, if instead of being written out in a straightforward fashion, the main idea is implied, just write in the margin the main idea as you understand it.

b. Once you have identified the main idea of the section you are reading, you need to be aware of how the author supports that main idea—the supporting details. As you come across supporting details, highlight, underline, or number them in the text and mark the margin with "SD" (supporting detail).

Repeat a. and b., above, until you finish the chapter.

2. After you have finished reading the chapter and noting the main ideas and supporting details, it is time to transfer those thoughts onto another surface, easily typed into your computer word processing program. Label all your main ideas (these should be **complete sentences**) with Roman numerals (I, II, III, IV, etc.) and under each main idea, list the corresponding supporting details, indented and with letters and numbers (a, b, c, 1,2,3, etc.). The supporting details should be in note form, not complete sentences. It should look like this:

I. Main idea of a section in a complete sentence
  A. supporting detail in note form
  B. supporting detail in note form
II. Main idea of a section in a complete sentence
  A. supporting detail in note form
      1. supporting detail in note form
      2. supporting detail in note form
  B. supporting detail in note form
  C. supporting detail in note form-

A good way of thinking about how to come up with the Roman numeral part—the main idea of the section in a complete sentence—is to **take the heading and combine it with what the section is generally about.**

3. The third part of this strategy is actually a **study strategy**: as you go back to review this chapter, try to recreate from memory your outline. Parts of the outline that you cannot recall indicate places in the text you may want to reread. The ability to reproduce the entire outline from memory is an indication that you have a good grasp of the chapter.

Below is the excerpt we looked at in the Structure Glance module. Consider how would you outline this section.

What is an Element?

An element is a pure substance that can not be broken down into simpler substances, with different properties, by physical or chemical means. The elements are the basic building blocks of all matter.

Three Types of Elements

Elements can be classified into three types, depending on their properties: metals, nonmetals, and metalloids.

Element Type 1: Metals

Examples of metallic elements are sodium (which has the symbol Na), calcium (Ca), iron (Fe), cobalt (Co), and silver (Ag). These elements are all classified as metals because they have luster, they conduct electricity well, they conduct heat well, and are malleable.

Element Type 2: Nonmetals

Some examples of nonmetals are chlorine, which has the symbol Cl, oxygen (O), carbon (C), and sulfur (S). These elements are classified as nonmetals because they don't shine, they don't conduct electricity well, they don't conduct heat well, and they are not malleable.

Element Type 3: Metalloids

Metalloids have some properties like those of metals and other properties like those of nonmetals. Some examples are arsenic (As), germanium (Ge), and silicon (Si). These particular metalloids are used in manufacturing transistors and other semiconductor devices.

Adapted from Nist & Diehl (2002), pp. 355-6

Your outline may look like this:

I. Main idea sentence
    A. Supporting details in note form
        1. example

I. *Elements are pure substances that can not be broken down into simpler substances.*
    A. *3 types of elements*
        1. *metals*
        2. *nonmetals*
        3. *metalloids*

> Outlining is a concise logical way to take notes as your read. You organize the information in the textbook as you locate main ideas and major supporting details.

Text Practice

Using the sample reading that follows, try this strategy on the practice textbook excerpt.

Note: this example begins with a prepared outline of the **entire** chapter. The sample reading is only **part** of the chapter.

1. Determine where the reading fits into the prepared outline.

2. Make a more elaborate outline of this reading.

Sample Reading for Module 7

Memory

Sample Reading for Module 11

Remembering, Disremembering, and Forgetting

The flipside of memory is **forgetting,** the inability to remember, Ebbinghaus (1885) documented over a century ago a typical pattern of forgetting that occurs with many kinds of declarative knowledge, beginning with rapid initial loss of information after initial learning and only gradual decline thereafter (Figure 6.18). Researchers have recently refined Ebbinghaus

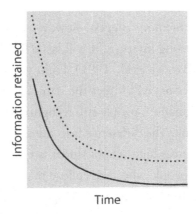

Time

Figure 6.18 Forgetting follows a standard pattern, with rapid initial loss of information followed by more gradual later decline. Increasing initial study-time (the dotted line) increases retention, but forgetting occurs at the same rate. In other words, increased study shifts the curve upward but does not change the rate of forgetting or eliminate it.

forgetting curve, finding that the relation between memory decline and length of time between learning and retrieval is logarithmic, which essentially beams that the rate of forgetting is initially very high but eventually becomes very low (Wilted & Ebbesen, 1991). Interestingly, this forgetting curve seems to apply whether the period of time is hours or years. The same curve emerged when researchers studied people's ability to remember the names of old television shows: They rapidly forgot the names of shows canceled within the last seven years, but the rate of forgetting trailed off after that (Squire, 1989).

How Long Is Long-Term Memory?

When people forget, does this mean that the information is no longer stored or simply that it is no longer easy to retrieve? And is some information permanent, or does the mind eventually throw away old boxes in the attic if the person does not use them for a number of years?

The first question is more difficult to answer than the second. Psychologists often distinguish between the *availability* of information in memory—whether it is still "in there"—and its *accessibility—the* ease with which it can be retrieved. The tip-of-the-tongue phenomenon, like the priming effects shown by amnesiacs, is a good example of information that is available but inaccessible. In large part, accessibility reflects level of activation, which diminishes over time but remains for much longer than most people would intuitively suppose. Memory for a picture flashed briefly on a screen a year earlier continues to have some amount of activation, which is expressed implicitly even if the person has no conscious recollection of it (Cave, 1997). And most people have vivid recollections of incidents from their childhood that occurred once, such as the moment they heard the news that a beloved pet died when they were six. But what about the other hundreds of millions of incidents that cannot be retrieved? To what degree these memories may now be unavailable, and not just inaccessible, is unknown.

Studies of very long term memory suggest, however, that if information is consolidated through spacing over long learning intervals, it will last a lifetime, even if the person does not rehearse it for half a century (Barrack et al., 1991). Eight years after having taught students for a single semester, college professors will forget the names and faces of most of their students (sorry!), but 35 years after graduation, people still recognize 90 percent of the names and faces from their high school yearbook. The difference is in the spacing: The professor only teaches a student for a few months, whereas high school students typically know each other for at least three or four years. Similarly, people who take college mathematics courses that require them to use the knowledge they learned in high school algebra show nearly complete memory for algebra 50 years later even if they work as artists and never balance their checkbook, whereas people who stop at high school algebra remember nothing of it decades later.

How Accurate Is Long-Term Memory?

Aside from the question of *how long* people remember is the question of *how accurately* they remember. The short answer is that if memory is both functional and reconstructive, most of the time it will serve us well, but it is subject to a variety of errors and biases. For example, the normal associative processes that help people remember can also lead to memory errors (see Robinson & Reedier, 1997; Schacter et al., 1998, in press). In one set of studies the researchers presented participants with a series of words (such as *slumber, nap,* and *bed)* that were all related to a single word that had *not* been presented *(sleep),* which essentially primed that word repeatedly (Reedier & McDermott, 1995). Not only did most participants "remember" having heard the multiply-primed word, but the majority even "remembered" which of two people had read the word to them. Some participants refused to believe that the word had not been presented even after hearing an audiotape of the session!

Emotional factors can also bias recall. The investigators in one study asked college student participants to recall their math, science, history, English, and foreign language grades from high school and then compared their recollections to their high school transcripts (Barrack et al., 1995). Students recalled 71 percent of their grades correctly. More interesting, however, was the pattern of their errors (Figure 6.19). Participants rarely disremembered their A's, but they rarely *correctly* remembered their D's. In fact, D's were twice more likely to be remembered as a B or a C than as a D. Approximately 80 percent of participants tended to inflate their remembered grades, whereas only 5 percent reported grades lower than they had actually achieved. The remaining 14 percent remembered correctly.

Flashbulb Memories

If remembering is more like consulting an artist's sketch than a photograph, what do we make of **flashbulb memories**, that is, vivid memories of exciting or highly consequential events (Brown & Kulik, 1977; Conway, 1995; Pillager, 1995; Wino-grad & Weisser, 1996)? Many people around the world can recall precisely where and when they heard the news of the death

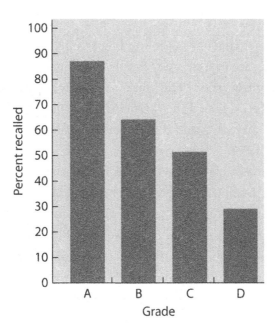

Figure 6.19 Distortion in memory for high school oracles. The lower the grade, the less memorable it seems to be, demonstrating the impact of motivation and emotion on memory. Source: Adapted from Barrack et al., 1996.

of Princess Diana of England in 1997, almost as if a camera had recorded that moment in time. People report similarly vivid memories of the assassination of Martin Luther King in 1968 as well as personal events such as the death of a loved one or a romantic encounter (Pillager, 1984; Rubin & Kozin, 1984).

Flashbulb memories are so clear and vivid that we tend to think of them as totally accurate; however, considerable evidence suggests that flashbulb memories are often not of snapshot clarity or accuracy and can even be entirely incorrect (Weisser, 1991). For people whose lives are directly affected, such as Princess Diana's children, flashbulb memories tend to be extremely accurate, especially for the central details of the episode. People who are only affected from afar, in contrast, tend to have much more confidence in their memories of vivid events than they should.

Eyewitness Testimony

Research on the accuracy of memory has an important real-life application in the courtroom: How accurate is eyewitness testimony (see Schaefer, 1995; Scorer et al., 1995)? Numerous studies have explored this question experimentally, usually by showing participants a short film or slides of an event such as a car accident (Loftus, 1979; Wells & Loftus, 1984; Wells & Turtle, 1987; Zaragosta & Mitchell, 1995). The experimenter then asks subjects specific questions about the scene, sometimes introducing information that was not present in the actual scene, asking leading questions, or contradicting what participants saw.

Even seemingly minor variations in the wording of a question can determine what participants "remember" from a scene. One study simply substituted the definite article "the" for the indefinite article "a" in the question "Did you see the/a broken headlight?" Using the definite article increased both the likelihood that participants would recall seeing a broken headlight and their certainty that they had, even if they never actually observed one (Loftus & Palmer, 1974; Loftus & Zanni, 1975).

These findings have clear implications both in the courtroom and in the way police interrogate witnesses, although some researchers have been unable to replicate these results or have qualified them on a number of grounds (e.g., Gruneberg & Sykes, 1996; Kohnken & Maass, 1988; McCloskey & Eget, 1986; Smith & Ellsworth, 1987; Yuille, 1980). For instance, individuals vary in their susceptibility to misleading information. People with poor memories are especially susceptible to misinformation (Loftus et al., 1992). Further, some aspects of a memory may be more reliable than others. The emotional stress of witnessing a traumatic event can lead to heightened processing (and hence better memory) of core details of the event but less extensive processing of peripheral details (Christianson, 1992). A sharp attorney could thus attack the credibility of a witness's entire testimony by establishing that her memory of peripheral details is faulty even though she clearly remembers the central aspects of the event.

INTERIM SUMMARY: The flipside of memory is **forgetting.** Many kinds of declarative knowledge show a similar forgetting curve, which is initially steep and then levels off. Psychologists often distinguish between the *availability* of information in memory—whether it is still "in there"—and its *accessibility—the* ease with which it can be retrieved. People tend to make memory errors for a variety of reasons, some cognitive and some emotional (such as remembering what they want to remember). **Flashbulb memories**—vivid memories of exciting or highly consequential events—are sometimes highly accurate but sometimes completely mistaken. Eyewitness testimony is also subject to many biases and errors, although people are more likely to remember central, emotionally significant details.

Why Do People Forget?

The reconstructive nature of remembering—the fact that we have to weave together a memory from patches of specific and general knowledge—leaves memory open to a number of potential errors and biases. But why do people sometimes forget things entirely? Psychologists have proposed several explanations, including decay, interference, and motivated forgetting.

Decay Theory

The **decay theory** explains forgetting as a result of a fading memory trace, having a thought or perception produces changes in synaptic connections, which in turn creates the potential for remembering if the neural circuits that were initially activated are later reactivated. According to decay theory, these neurophysiological changes fade with disuse, much as a wilderness path grows over unless repeatedly trodden. The decay theory is difficult to corroborate or disprove empirically, but some studies show a similar pattern of rapid and then more gradual deactivation of neural pathways in the hippocampus, which is involved in memory consolidation, suggesting a possible physiological basis for decay (see Anderson, 1995).

Interference Theory

A second theory points to **interference** as the prime culprit in memory failure of similar information or events tend to interfere with one another, as when students confuse two theories they learned about around the same time or two similar-sounding words in a foreign language. Finding the right path in the neural wilderness is difficult if two paths are close together and look alike. Or to use the filing cabinet metaphor, storing too many documents under the same heading makes finding the right one difficult.

Cognitive psychologists distinguish two kinds of interference. **Proactive interference** refer to the interference of previously stored memories with the retrieval of new information, as when a person calls a new romantic partner by the name of an old one (a common but dangerous memory lapse). In **retroactive interference,** new information interferes with retrieval of old information, as when people have difficulty recalling their home phone numbers from past residences. One reason children take years to memorize multiplication tables, even though they can learn the names of cartoon characters or classmates with astonishing speed, is the tremendous interference involved, because every number is paired with so many others (Anderson, 1995).

Motivated Forgetting

Another cause of forgetting is motivated forgetting or forgetting for a reason. People often explicitly instruct themselves or others to forget, as when a person stops in the middle of a sentence and says, "Oops—forget that. That's the wrong address. The right one is …" (Bork & Bork, 1995). At other times, the "intention" to forget is implicit, as when a person who parks in the same garage everyday implicitly *remembers to forget* where she parked the day before so it does not interfere with memory for where she parked today (Bjork, et *al.,* 1998). Experimental evidence suggests that this kind of goal-directed forgetting requires active inhibition of the forgotten information, which remains active but inaccessible. Researchers have demonstrated this using *directed forgetting* procedures, in which participants learn a list of words but are told midway through to forget the words they just learned and just remember the last part of the list. This procedure reduces recall for the words in the first part of the list and decreases proactive interference from them, so that words in the last half of the list are more easily remembered. This suggests that the procedure is in fact inhibiting retrieval of the to-be-forgotten words. On the other hand, this procedure does *not* decrease recognition of, or implicit memory for, the to-be-forgotten words, suggesting that they remain in an activated state.

Other studies show that instructing a person not to think about something can effectively keep the information from consciousness but that doing so creates an automatic, unconscious process that "watches out" for the information and hence keeps it active (Wegner, 1992). For example, when people are instructed to suppress an exciting thought about sex, they remain physiologically aroused even while the thought is outside awareness. In fact, they remain just as aroused as subjects instructed to *think about* the sexual thought (Wegner et al., 1990). In a sense, goal-directed forgetting is like a form of prospective memory, in which the intention is to forget something in the future rather than to remember it.

In real life, people often try to inhibit unpleasant or anxiety-provoking thoughts or feelings. When they do this consciously, as when they tell themselves not to worry about a medical procedure they are about to undergo, it is called *suppression*. When they do this unconsciously, it is called *repression* [...]. People often forget things they do not want to remember, such as "overlooking" a dentist appointment. If dentists were handing out $100 bills instead of filling teeth, few people would forget their appointments.

...And, as you go out into the world, I predict that you will, gradually and imperceptibly, forget all you ever learned at this university.

Your Text

Try this strategy on a chapter from your content area class that you need to read this week.

CHAPTER: **PAGES:**

> Outlining as a reading strategy is the exact opposite of outlining as a writing strategy. As a reading strategy, the 'paper' has already been written and it is your job to deconstruct it down to the basics.

Strategy Feedback Prompt

This exercise is meant to be reflective in nature as you consider how you liked the strategy. Finish completing the prompt **after** you apply the strategy to your content area textbook.

> Learning to think about what works for you is important as you take command of your learning.

Module #:
Module Name:

Describe how to do the strategy in detail:

Chapter title and number worked on today:

Outcome: Write a paragraph about your use of the strategy with your own textbook. Comment on the following and add any other thoughts that you would like to share: *How well did the strategy work on your own textbook chapter? Did you have to adjust the strategy when applying it to your own textbook chapter? How? What did you get out of this module?*

Mastery Assessment

The Mastery Assessment for this module involves deconstructing a textbook reading as you create the outline.

You will need to assess your learning in order to discover your strengths and weaknesses.

Module 12

Sidebar Summaries

Introduction

The purpose of this module is to encourage you to read and understand the sidebars. Sidebars are the added information that is printed in the margin of some texts. The author of your text may have attempted to help you understand the text by providing abbreviated notes in the margins. Usually these notes are boxed in some way to separate themselves from the rest of the text. Sidebars are different from pictures, charts, and graphs because they contain no graphics—just mini summaries of what is important. These sidebars are excellent ways to see what is in the chapter, what is important in a chapter, and what to study.

> Sidebars help make the text significant and meaningful in your life.

Step-by-Step Strategy Description

1. Choose a chapter for focus.
2. Identify all the sidebars.
3. Make 2 columns on your paper. In the first column, list the information in the sidebar. In the second column, explain this information in your own words. For any sidebar that you do not understand, you will find a lengthier explanation of it within the text. If the sidebars are just definitions, try giving an example of each to show that you understand the definition.

> Relating to the sidebars can give you a broad knowledge base on a particular subject that will make the subject easier to read.

Using the sample reading that follows, try this strategy on the practice textbook excerpt.

> Gather data, ponder, analyze, and/or make conclusions as you consider the connections of the sidebars to the content in the reading.

Information in the sidebar	*Explain the sidebar using your own words. For any sidebar that you do not understand, you will find a lengthier explanation in the text to help you. Add examples for a more complete study tool.*

Sample Reading for Module 12

At what point does a creature become categorized as "human"?

Prototypes: People typically classify object rapidly by judging their similarity to concepts stored in memory (Estes, 1994 Tvrsky, 1977). For example, if asked whether Windor, Ontario, is a city, most people compare it with their image of a crowded, bustling, typical ex-ample of a city, such as New York City, or with a generalized portrait extracted from experience with several cities, such s Los Angeles, Toronto, New York, and London.

> Finding similarities in concepts helps to categorize the concepts.

> People readily recognize robins as birds because it is a prototypical bird.

> Why does categorizing penguins take a little longer?

Researchers have learned how people use similarity in classification by using both visual and verbal categorization tasks. In visual categorization tasks, the experimenter states the name of a target category (e.g., *bird*) and then presents a picture and asks whether it is a member of the category. In verbal categorization tasks, the target category is followed by a word instead of a picture (e.g., *sparrow)*', the task for the subject is to judge whether the second word is an instance of the category.

Psychologists have learned about the role of similarity in classification by measuring the time subjects take to respond in tasks such as these. For example, people rapidly recognize that a robin is a bird but take 100 to 200 milliseconds longer to classify a penguin (see Smith, 1995). The reason is that a robin is a more *prototypical* bird, that is, it shares more of the characteristic features of the concept (Rosch, 1978).

A prototype represents a category. The prototype of a bird would represent all birds: robins, bluebirds, and sparrows, etc.

Prototypical features are the similar features found in all members of a prototype. For example, for the prototype birds, the prototypical features are: fly, sing, have wings, lay eggs.

A **prototype** is an abstraction across many instances of a category (such as robins, bluebirds, and sparrows). When people construct a prototype in their minds, they essentially abstract out the most important common features of the objects in a category. Thus, the prototype of a bird does not look exactly like any particular bird the person has ever seen; it is more like an airbrushed photograph that smooths out idiosyncratic features.

When people judge similarity in visual tasks, they rely primarily on shape. When they judge similarity verbally, they tend to rely on characteristic or prototypical features, that is, qualities typically found in members of a category. For example, most birds fly, sing, and lay eggs. People classify robins quickly because they do all three. Penguins take longer to classify because they lay eggs but do not share many other features of birds, except for having wings (see Malt & Smith, 1984). Most concepts include both visual information and information about characteristic features, so that in everyday categorization, people often use some combination of the two.

Your text

Try this strategy on a chapter from your content area class that you need to read this week. If the chapter does not contain sidebars, you will have to make your own sidebars.

CHAPTER: **PAGES:**

Information in the sidebar	*Explain the sidebar using your own words. For any sidebar that you do not understand, you will find a lengthier explanation in the text to help you. Add examples for a more complete study tool.*

Strategy Feedback Prompt

This exercise is meant to be reflective in nature as you consider how you liked the strategy. Finish completing the prompt after you apply the strategy to your content area textbook.

Module #:
Module Name:

Describe how to do the strategy in detail:

Chapter title and number worked on today:

Outcome: Write a paragraph about your use of the strategy with your own textbook. Comment on the following and add any other thoughts that you would like to share: *How well did the strategy work on your own textbook chapter? Did you have to adjust the strategy when applying it to your own textbook chapter? How? What did you get out of this module?*

Mastery Assessment

Some textbooks have huge sidebars. Some textbooks have none. The Mastery Assessment for this module involves deconstructing a textbook reading as you make sidebars. Create seven sidebars from a chosen reading.

1.

2.

3.

4.

5.

6.

7.

GRAPHIC ORGANIZERS

Sidebars are just another form of a graphic organizer that helps you construct meaning as you read your chapter. Other examples of graphic organizers include outlines, concept maps, flow charts, power point slides, trains, maps, timelines, trees, human figures, house, etc. Think about the steps you follow when you make a graphic organizer. Think about the similarities in how they might help you with comprehension.

List the similarities in function and in the process of making graphic organizers:

1.

2.

3.

4.

5.

6.

Show what each looks like. If you need to use the web to look them up, copy the web address for reference and citation purposes.

OUTLINE

CONCEPT MAP

FLOW CHART

POWER POINT SLIDE

TRAIN

SIDEBAR SUMMARY

HUMAN FIGURE

MAP

TREE

HOUSE

Module 13

Concept Mapping

Introduction

Concept Mapping is similar to outlining, in that you are writing down main ideas and supporting details in a format that reveals their relationship. But for many people, Concept Mapping frees them from the more rigid format of outlining that can seem un-natural at times. **Concept Mapping is a more free flowing, less structured study aid that still allows you to focus on the important aspects of the chapter.**

> Concept Mapping helps you make a tangible visual representation of the main ideas in the reading.

Step by Step Strategy Directions

As you read for new information and differentiate between the main ideas and the primary support in each section, you will need to determine the connection between ideas.

1. In the middle of a sheet of paper, write down a **key word or phrase that represents the overriding topic of the chapter**, and circle that word/phrase:

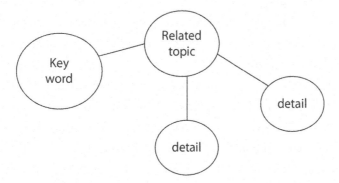

2. As you come across other important ideas, think about how they relate to this central idea. Write them down in another circle, and connect them to the original circle:

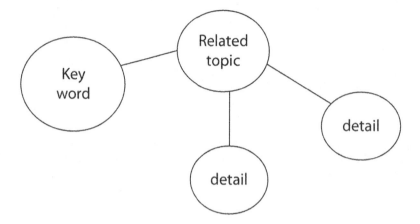

The idea here is to **work quickly**, without overanalyzing the relationships, to try and map out the chapter.

3. After you have finished reading the chapter and mapping out its central ideas, go back and look at your map. Do the connections make sense? What is your "picture" of the chapter? If necessary, reorganize and redraw your map to make the concepts clearer. Reread sections and add examples to your map in places where you are not clear of that section's information.

Example

The States of Matter

Matter may exist in any of the three physical states: solid, liquid, and gas.

A solid has a definite shape and volume that it tends to maintain under normal conditions. The particles composing a solid stick rigidly to one another. Solids most commonly occur in the crystalline form, which means they have a fixed, regularly repeating, symmetrical internal structure. Diamonds, salt, and quartz are examples of crystalline solids. A few solids, such as glass and paraffin, do not have a well-defined crystalline structure, although they do have a definite shape and volume. Such solids are called amorphous solids, which means they have no definite internal structure or form.

A liquid has a definite volume but does not have its own shape since it takes the shape of the container in which it is placed. Its particles cohere firmly, but not rigidly, so the particles of a liquid have a great deal of mobility while maintaining close contact with each other.

A gas has no fixed shape or volume and eventually spreads out to fill its container. As the gas particles move about they collide with the walls of their container causing *pressure*, which is a force exerted over an area. Gas particles move independently of one another.

Adapted from Nist & Diehl (2002), pp. 352

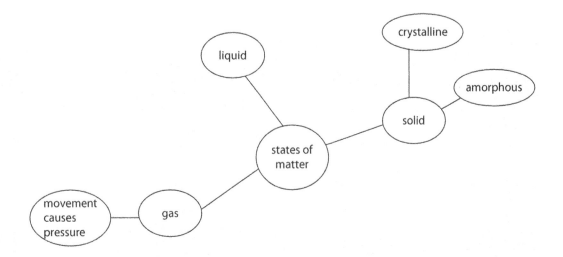

Text Practice

Using the sample reading that follows, try this strategy on the practice textbook excerpt.

> Rereading your concept map is a useful strategy to help you review the chapter. A good way to make sure that it makes sense is to try to explain it to someone else.

Sample Reading for Module 13

The Nature of Consciousness

Consciousness, the subjective awareness of mental events, may be easier to describe than to define. William James (1890) viewed consciousness as a constantly moving stream of thoughts, feelings, and perceptions. Shutting off consciousness in this sense is probably impossible, as anyone knows who has ever tried to "stop thinking" to escape insomnia. Following in the footsteps of the French philosopher Rene Descartes, who offered the famous proposition *"cogito ergo sum"* (I think, therefore I am), James also emphasized a second aspect of consciousness, the consciousness of self. James argued that part of being conscious of any particular thought is a simultaneous awareness of oneself as the author or owner of it.

Functions of Consciousness

Why do people have consciousness at all? Two of its functions are readily apparent. Consciousness monitors the self and the environment and controls thoughts and behavior (Kihlstrom, 1987). *Consciousness as a monitor* is analogous to a continuously moving video camera, surveying potentially significant perceptions, thoughts, emotions, goals, and problem-solving strategies. The *control function of consciousness* allows people to initiate and terminate thought and behavior in order to attain goals. People often rehearse scenarios in their minds, such as asking for a raise or confronting a disloyal friend. Consciousness is frequently engaged when people choose between competing strategies for solving a problem (Mandler & Nakamura, 1987).

These two functions of consciousness—monitoring and controlling—are intertwined, since consciousness monitors inner and outer experience in order to prevent and solve problems. For example, consciousness often "steps in" when automatized processes (procedural knowledge) are not successful. In this sense, consciousness is like the inspector in a garment factory: It does not make the product, but it checks to make sure the product is made correctly. If it finds an imperfection, it institutes a remedy (Gilbert, 1989, p. 206). In typing this sentence, for example, I paid no conscious attention to the keys on my terminal, but when I made a mistake—hitting an "m" instead of a comma, the adjacent key—I looked at the keys and corrected the error.

From an evolutionary standpoint, consciousness probably evolved as a mechanism for directing behavior in adaptive ways that was superimposed on more primitive psychological processes such as conditioning (Reber, 1992). Indeed, William James was heavily influenced by Darwin, and he explained consciousness in terms of its function: fostering adaptation. Consciousness is often "grabbed" by things that are unexpected, unusual, or contrary to expectations—precisely the things that could affect well-being or survival. Much of the time people respond automatically to the environment, learning and processing information without conscious awareness. Important choices, however, require more consideration, and consciousness permits heightened reflection on significant events and the likely consequences of alternative choices.

Interim summary: Consciousness refers to the subjective awareness of mental events. States of consciousness are qualitatively different patterns of subjective experience, including ways of experiencing both internal and external events. Consciousness plays at least two functions: monitoring the self and the environment and controlling thought and behavior. Consciousness probably evolved as a mechanism for directing behavior in adaptive ways that was superimposed on more primitive psychological processes that today continue outside awareness.

Consciousness and Attention

At any given time, people are dimly aware of much more than what is conscious. For example, while reading the newspaper a person may have some vague awareness of the radiator clanking, voices in the next room, and the smell of breakfast cooking, although none of these is at the center of awareness or consciousness. At some point, however, certain olfactory sensations may unconsciously be given enough perceptual meaning (smoke or danger) to shift attention. Paradoxically, the monitoring and controlling functions of consciousness are thus to a considerable degree regulated *outside* of consciousness, by unconscious or implicit attentional mechanisms that focus conscious awareness.

Attention

Attention refers to the process of focusing conscious awareness, providing heightened sensitivity to a limited range of experience requiring more expensive information processing. *Selection*—of a particular object, a train of thought, or a location in space at which something important might be happening—is the essence of attention (Rees et al., 1997). Attention is generally guided by some combination of external stimulation—which naturally leads us to focus on relevant sensory information—and activated goals—which lead us to attend to thoughts, feelings, or stimuli relevant to obtaining them.

Filtering in and Filtering out Some psychologists have likened attention to a filtering process through which only more important information passes (Broadbent, 1958). For example, people frequently become so engrossed in conversation with one person that they tune out all the other conversations in the room—an important skill at a loud party. However, if they hear someone mention their name across the room, they may suddenly look up and focus attention on the person who has just spoken the magic word. This phenomenon, called the *cocktail party phenomenon* (Cherry, 1953), suggests that we implicitly process much more information than reaches consciousness.

On the other hand, people also sometimes divert attention from information that may be relevant but emotionally upsetting, a process called selective inattention. This can be highly adaptive, as when students divert their attention from the anxiety of taking a test to the task itself. It can also be maladaptive, as when people ignore something as small as a darkening birthmark on the arm or as global as nuclear proliferation and hence fail to devote adequate cognitive resources to them (Lifton, 1980).

Components of Attention Attention actually consists of at least three functions : *orienting to* sensory stimuli, *controlling the contents* of consciousness and voluntary behavior, *and maintaining alertness* (see Posner, 1995). Different neural networks (using different neurotransmitter systems) appear to be involved in these three functions (Robbins, 1997). Orienting, which has been studied most extensively in the visual system (Rafal & Robertson, 1995), involves turning sensory organs such as the eyes and ears toward a stimulus. It also involves spreading extra activation to the parts of the cortex that are processing information about the stimulus and probably inhibiting activation of others. When we attend to a stimulus, such as a mosquito buzzing around the room, the brain uses the same circuits it normally uses to process information that is not the focus of attention. For example, watching the mosquito leads to activation of the "what" and "where" visual pathways in the occipital, temporal, and parietal lobes. Attention enhances processing at those cortical locations as soon as a person (or monkey) has been signaled to watch or listen for particular stimuli or stimuli in a specific location. Recent PET data suggest that attentional mechanisms may generally increase the activation of a particular region of the brain when a person or monkey is signaled to watch for a stimulus; attentional mechanisms may also spread extra activation to objects once detected so they can be examined more carefully (Rees et al., 1997).

Controlling the contents of consciousness (such as deciding how much to listen to something someone is saying) and controlling voluntary behavior involve different neural pathways than orienting to stimuli. These "executive" control functions typically involve areas of the frontal lobes and basal ganglia, which are known to be involved in thought, movement, and self-control. In contrast, orienting to stimuli tends to require the involvement of neural circuits in the midbrain (such as the superior colliculus, which helps control eye movements), thalamus (which directs attention to particular sensory systems), and parietal lobes (which, among other functions, direct attention to particular locations).

Maintaining alertness is crucial in tasks ranging from paying attention to items on a test—and ignoring distractions such as anxiety or the sounds of traffic outside—to staying alert enough to notice a small change while keeping an eye on a radar screen for hours. A whole network of neurons from the reticular formation (which is involved in regulating states of alertness) through the frontal lobes appear to regulate alertness (Posner, 1995).

Divided Attention

Everyone has had the experience of trying to pay attention to too many things at once—and consequently not understanding or competently performing any of them. Psychologists have tried to determine the extent to which whether people can split attention between two complex tasks, such as following two conversations simultaneously; this is known as divided attention (see Craik et al., 1996). One way researchers study divided attention is through dichotic listening tasks [...]: Subjects are fitted with earphones, and different information is directed into each ear simultaneously. They are instructed to attend only to the information from one ear by repeating aloud what they hear in that ear for a period of time, a process called *shadowing*. Attending to one channel or the other is difficult at first; it is easier if the two channels differ in topic, voice pitch, and so forth (Hirst, 1986).

Subjects can become so adept at shadowing that they are completely unable to recognize information in the unattended channel, performing no better than chance when asked whether a word presented in the unattended channel had been presented. Nevertheless, the information does appear to be processed to some degree, much as the smell of smoke is processed while reading a newspaper. This has been clearly demonstrated in research on priming [...], the process by which exposure to a stimulus (such as a word) affects performance on tasks involving related stimuli (Nisbett & Wilson, 1977; Schacter, 1992). For example, a subject who hears "England" in the unattended channel may have no recollection of having heard the name of any country. When compared to a control subject who has not been similarly primed, however, the individual is more likely to say "London" if asked to name a capital city, and he will more quickly fill in the missing letters when asked for the name of a city when presented with

LO _ _ _ N.

The data from many dichotic listening studies of divided attention actually suggest that subjects may not be dividing their attention at all: Failing to show recognition memory for the prime suggests that participants never consciously attended to it. In other cases, however, people do appear to divide their attention, performing two complex tasks simultaneously. Listening to a lecture while taking notes requires a student to hear and process one idea while simultaneously writing, and even paraphrasing, a previous idea or sentence. This is remarkable because both tasks are verbal and the content of each is highly similar; hence, one would expect heavy interference between the two. Psychologists have even trained subjects to take dictation while reading (Spelke et al., 1976).

Sometimes people accomplish such feats by rapidly shifting attention back and forth between the two tasks. Much of the time, however, people solve attentional dilemmas by automatizing one task or the other [...]. Automatization develops through practice, as actions previously performed with deliberate conscious effort are eventually processed automatically. While students listen to a lecture, their primary focus of consciousness is on the lecturer's current words, while a largely automatic process, perhaps drawing on some subset of attentional processes, allows note taking. Precisely how much consciousness is involved in divided attention is not well understood. Students can generally recount what they have just written even while listening to a lecture, suggesting *some* involvement of conscious attention, although their primary allocation of attentional resources is to the lecturer

Interim Summary: Attention refers to the process of focusing conscious awareness, providing heightened sensitivity to a limited range of experience requiring more extensive information processing. Attention consists of at least three functions: orienting to sensory stimuli, controlling the contents of consciousness and voluntary behavior, and maintaining alertness. **Divided attention**, which often involves automatizing one or more tasks or rapidly shifting attention between them, refers to the capacity to split attention or cognitive resources between two or more tasks.

The Normal Flow of Consciousness

A major component of the normal flow of consciousness is **daydreaming**—turning attention away from external stimuli to internal thoughts and imagined scenarios. Some daydreams are pleasurable fantasies, whereas others involve planning for future actions, particularly involving people in important relationships. In one large-scale study of daydreaming, all subjects reported daydreaming daily (Singer, 1975). Another research team found that college students daydream about half the time they are conscious, if daydreaming includes thoughts about something other than what is currently happening in the person's environment, such as thinking about a paper that needs to be written while watching a basketball game or engaging in a less than captivating conversation (Klinger, 1992).

Psychologists study the normal flow of consciousness through **experience-sampling** techniques (Larsen, 1997; Singer & Kolligian, 1987; Wong & Csikszentmihalyi, 1991). In one design, subjects talk aloud, sometimes while performing a task, simply reporting the contents of their consciousness. Psychologists then code their verbal responses into categories, such as emotional tone, relevance to the task at hand, or content.

Beeper Studies

An experience-sampling technique that has provided a more natural window to the flow of consciousness in everyday life is used in beeper studies, in which participants carry pagers and report their experience when "beeped" at various points during the day. In one study, researchers sampled the experience of 75 adolescents from a Chicago high school (Csikszentmihalyi & Larson, 1984). They randomly selected students within each of several categories, including sex, grade, and social class (a stratified random sample […]). For one week, participants were beeped at some point during every two-hour period (except, of course, at night), at which time they filled out a brief form reporting what they were doing and with whom, what they were thinking and feeling, and how intensely they were feeling it.

Some of the results were quite unexpected. When subjects were with their families, their negative thoughts outnumbered their positive thoughts by about 10 to 1. When they were asked, "As you were beeped, what were you thinking about?" their responses included "my aunt talks too much" or "how incompetent my mom is" (p. 139). Using this method, the investigators were also able to explore the subjective experience of individual subjects […].

Culture and Consciousness

We are accustomed to thinking of consciousness as a realm of experience that is uniquely private, but consciousness is in part culturally constructed. Cultural practices and beliefs shape the way people organize their subjective world, including the way they conceive of time and space (Hallowell, 1955; Shore, 1996). In most preindustrial cultures, consciousness is organized into broad units of time, such as sunup and sundown, rather than into the tiny units of time that organize consciousness in cultures ruled by the clock.

Cultural processes also shape the phenomena to which people turn their attention. People in the industrialized West are constantly making inferences about other people's mental states, listening carefully to their words and actions to try to figure out, for example, whether they are sincere—that is, whether they really *mean* what they are saying. In contrast, the Ifaluk of Micronesia, like many preindustrialized peoples, are not so concerned with the inner meanings of social actions (Lutz, 1992). Their moral code revolves around harmony within the group, which is essential for people who must live together on a small island. When people are behaving in ways that maintain this harmony, no one is concerned about whether or not they mean it, since the Ifaluk assume that people behave morally because that is the right thing to do. Further, the kind of introspection valued in many segments of contemporary Western culture, which involves self-reflection for the purpose of self-knowledge, is not encouraged by Ifaluk values and practices. In fact, the Ifaluk perceive it as a sign of self-absorption (Lutz, 1992).

INTERIM SUMMARY Prominent in the normal flow of conscious experience are **day** dreams, in which the person turns attention away from external stimuli to internal thoughts and imagined scenarios, often for pleasure or for problem solving. Psychologists learn about the normal flow of consciousness through **experience-sampling** techniques, such as beeper studies, in which participants carry pagers and report on aspects of consciousness when they are paged at random intervals. Cultural practices and beliefs shape the way people organize their conscious experience, including the way they conceive of time and space and the extent to which they focus on their own and others' internal states.

Perspectives on Consciousness

Consciousness occupied a central role in the first textbook on psychology, written by William James in 1890, and figured prominently in the work of Freud, who expanded the focus of psychology to include unconscious processes as well. When behaviorism came into ascendance, consciousness as a focus of investigation receded from the consciousness of the scientific community and remained that way until the 1980s. Behaviorists wanted to avoid explaining behaviors in terms of mental events that cannot be observed scientifically, since people's introspective reports are impossible to verify. Behaviorists also rejected the idea of a conscious mind as an agent that chooses, intends, or makes decisions (Skinner, 1974, p. 169). Organisms as primitive as snails respond to environmental contingencies, yet no one would propose that snails therefore have consciousness. Further, according to Skinner, to explain a person's action on the basis of an unconscious process is simply to admit that we have not yet observed the environmental stimuli controlling the behavior.

Until about a decade ago, cognitive psychologists paid little attention to consciousness, either. But as we saw [...] that all changed with the surge of research on implicit memory and cognition. In the last decade, spurred by developments in neuroscience and neuro-imaging that provide a new window *on* consciousness, cognitive scientists—as well as philosophers, neurologists, biologists, and even physicists—have begun rethinking consciousness (e.g., Edelman, 1989; Cohen & Schooler, 1997). In this section we examine psychodynamic and cognitive perspectives on consciousness and explore ways they converge. We then consider what can be learned about normal consciousness by observing neuropsychological patients like Claparede's, who manifest dissociation between what they know consciously and unconsciously.

The Psychodynamic Unconscious

Freud (1900) defined consciousness as one of three mental systems called the conscious, preconscious, and unconscious [...]. **Conscious** mental processes are those of which a person is subjectively aware (such as the sentence you just read—if you were paying attention!). **Preconscious m**ental processes are not presently conscious but –could be readily brought to consciousness if the need arose, such as the smell of bacon cooking in the background or the name of a city that is not currently in mind but could easily be retrieved. **Unconscious processes** are inaccessible to consciousness because–they would be too anxiety provoking to acknowledge; that is, they are repressed.

Freud likened repression to a censor: Just as a repressive government censors ideas or wishes it considers threatening, so, too, does the mind censor threatening thoughts from consciousness

[...]. Thus, a person may remember an abusive father with love and admiration and have little access to unhappy memories because admitting the truth would be painful. Unconscious processes of this sort are *dynamically unconscious*—that is, kept unconscious for a reason, requiring psychological effort or energy (dynamic force) to keep them out of awareness. Freud (1915) recognized that many other psychological processes are *descriptively unconscious—that* is, not conscious even though they are not threatening, such as the processes by which depletion of glucose levels in the blood lead to hunger.

Subliminal Perception

In the 1940s and 1950s, as part of the New Look in perception [...] researchers tested hypotheses derived from Freud's Theory of consciousness. Studies of **subliminal perception**-the perception of stimuli below the threshold of consciousness—used a device called *a tachistoscope* to flash images, too quickly for conscious recognition but slowly enough to be registered outside awareness (Dixon, 1971, 1981; Erdelyi, 1985; Weinberger, in press). For example, in one study the experimenter flashed one of two pictures subliminally [...]. The first depicted a boy behaving aggressively toward a man; the second depicted the boy presenting a man with a birthday cake. Participants were then shown a neutral picture of the boy and asked to judge the boy's personality. Participants exposed to the aggressive picture tended to judge the boy negatively, whereas those who had been flashed the altruistic picture rated him positively.

This line of research drew considerable fire, in part because of methodological concerns, but also in part because the field was still dominated by behaviorism and was not yet ready for the concept of unconscious processes. In recent years, however, both psychodynamic and cognitive researchers have breathed new life into subliminal research, demonstrating that subliminal presentation of stimuli can indeed influence thought and emotion (Bowers, 1984; Neidenthal & Cantor, 1986; Shevrin et al., 1996; Weinberger & Hardaway, 1990). For instance, subliminal presentation of a happy or sad face directly prior to exposure to a novel visual stimulus (such as a Chinese letter) affects the extent to which subjects like it (Murphy & Zajonc, 1993). Subliminal presentations of the face seems to "tag" the stimulus with an emotional connotation.

In one study, the investigator subliminally presented participants with either a word or blank field (Marcel, 1983). The stimulus was followed immediately by a masking stimulus to prevent it from lingering as a visual memory.

Your Text

Try this strategy on a chapter from your content area class that you need to read this week.
CHAPTER: **PAGES:**

> Concept mapping shows proof that you understand the reading as you demonstrate the connection of ideas. Presenting your map to others is a form of review as you talk about the content.

Strategy Feedback Prompt

This reflection to be finished after you apply the strategy to your content area textbook.

> Learning to think about what works for you is important as you take command of your learning.

Module #:
Module Name:

Describe how to do the strategy in detail:

Chapter title and number worked on today:

Outcome: Write a paragraph about your use of the strategy with your own textbook. Comment on the following and add any other thoughts that you would like to share: *How well did the strategy work on your own textbook chapter? Did you have to adjust the strategy when applying it to your own textbook chapter? How? What did you get out of this module?*

Mastery Assessment

The Mastery Assessment for this module involves making a concept map of a chosen reading.

> You will need to assess your learning in order to discover your strengths and weaknesses.

Module 14

Introduction/Conclusion Breakdown

Introduction

The purpose of this module is to help you determine the main concepts of a chapter. With this strategy you are noting the main topics so that when you begin reading the chapter, you can recognize the supporting details.

> The introduction and conclusion of a chapter incorporates all the elements of the chapter that you will need to know.

An introduction to a chapter is included to introduce the topics in order to help lead you through the chapter so that you know what to expect. The conclusion, or summary, to a chapter is included to help you recognize all the topics within the chapter that you should have noted when reading. By breaking down both the introduction and conclusion, you will be able to easily identify what is important and what to study. As you create your list of main ideas, you will be able to note the connection to supporting details while you are reading.

Step-by-Step Strategy Description

1. Choose a chapter for focus.
2. As you read the introduction, list the main topics that are presented.
3. As you read the conclusion, list the main topics that are presented.
4. Read the chapter, heading by heading, and explain each main topic as it is presented.
5. Optional: Add page numbers to your information to help you find it later when you need to review it for a test.

> The introduction and conclusion will help you note how a chapter is organized and will broaden your understanding of the chapter.

Using the sample reading that follows, complete only the Main Topics* column. The Supporting Details column will be incomplete because the rest of the chapter is not included in the sample.

When you finish, compare your work with others.

This strategy can be the starting point for your chapter. By reading the introduction and the conclusion first you can bring in any prior knowledge that you have in order to make connections to the reading.

Main Topics*
List the main topics in the introduction and conclusion

Supporting Details
Fill in details as you read the chapter section by section

_____
_____
_____
_____
_____
_____
_____
_____
_____
_____
_____
_____
_____
_____
_____
_____
_____
_____
_____
_____
_____
_____
_____

Sample Reading for Module 14

*This is the **introduction** of a chapter on emotion, stress, and coping.*

Emotion, Stress, and Coping

In March of 1998, the media in the United States were aflurry with reports of a Presidential sex scandal. For years, allegations of affairs had surrounded President Clinton, but they had taken on new intensity since January when a story broke suggesting an affair between the President and a 21-year-old White House intern named Monica Lewinsky. The public, however, had already begun to forgive the popular President, as evidenced in record-high approval ratings, assuming that even if he had dallied with the intern, the relationship was seedy but consensual.

But in March, a new story broke when Kathleen Willey, a former supporter of the President, alleged in front of a television audience of 20 million that the President had forced himself on her in the Oval Office—kissing her, fondling her, and putting her hand on his body. Her televised performance was, in the words of many commentators, "mesmerizing." She spoke with a combination of pain and composure, speaking articulately with emotional pauses that seemed to indicate a compelling story. Perhaps even more compelling was the lack of a motive for anything but honesty. After all, she had been in the Clinton camp for years.

A day later, however, another side of the story began to emerge. The White House released copies of letters she had written the President many times after the alleged incident, in which she asked for private appointments with him, sent him birthday and other congratulatory cards, and described herself as his "number one fan." More damning still was the presence of a possible motive: Her lawyer had been busy arranging a $300,000 book deal, an amount that would virtually cancel out a debt with which her deceased husband had left her.

In the days surrounding the incident, after watching the dozens of "talking heads" on television, my graduate student Ali Feit and I were struck by how much the inferences these commentators made about the case seemed to depend on their political preferences. Republicans described Willey's emotional testimony as highly credible; Democrats pointed to the book negotiations as clear evidence of her motive for lying. How could people vary so widely in their inferences after seeing exactly the same interview?

To try to answer that question, in the next three days we distributed questionnaires to roughly 120 people in Boston and New York asking them about what they thought had happened between the President and Mrs. Willey, as well as assessing their feelings toward Democrats, Republicans, feminists, Clinton, and infidelity. We also assessed their knowledge of Clinton's life and the current scandal, so that we could test the hypothesis that people's inferences in ambiguous, emotionally charged incidents of this sort reflect a combination of cognitive processes (based on their prior knowledge) and emotional pulls.

That was just what we found. We used a statistical procedure (called *multiple regression*) that can determine how much of one variable (in this case, the extent to which participants believed

Clinton had forced himself on Willey) can be accounted for by other variables (in this instance, feelings about Republicans and Democrats, knowledge about Clinton, etc.). The best predictor of beliefs about what happened between the President and Mrs. Willey was people's feelings to-ward the two political parties: The more strongly people liked Republicans, the more strongly they believed the President had sexually harassed Willey. The second strongest predictor was feelings about high-status philandering men: People who strongly disliked =faithful, charismatic men also tended to believe Willey's account. A somewhat distant third was people's knowledge about Clinton's life: The more they knew, the more they thought he did it.

This example raises many of the questions that will emerge in this chapter on emotion, stress, and coping. What emotional cues help us decipher whether a person is lying or telling the -truth? Is our ability to read those cues inborn? How does emotion affect cognition? And how do people cope with stressful events, such as unwanted sexual advances or public attacks on their character? We begin by exploring the nature of emotion, starting with components and types of emotion and different perspectives on emotional experience. Next, we turn to the related phenomenon of stress, from major stresses like the death of a spouse, to catastrophes like earthquakes, to daily hassles like traffic and sloppy roommates. After examining stress and its effects on health, we explore the strategies people use to cope with stress, as well as the role of culture in patterning responses to experiences ranging from loss and unemployment to discrimination and torture.

Emotion

Everyone has an intuitive sense of what an emotion is, but emotion can be exceedingly difficult to define. Imagine explaining the concept of emotion to some-one who has never experienced one (like a tax collector). Emotion, or affect (a synonym for emotion, pronounced with the ac-cent on the first syllable), is an evaluative response (a positive or negative feeling) that typically includes some combination of physiological arousal, subjective experience, and behavioral or emotional expression. We examine each component of emotion in turn.

Physiological Components

Over a century ago, William James (1884) argued that emotion is rooted in bodily experi-ence. According to James, an emotion-inducing stimulus elicits visceral, or gut, reactions and voluntary behaviors such as running or gesturing. The physical experience in turn leads the person to feel aroused, and the arousal stimulates the subjective experience of fear. In this view, confronting a bear on a camping trip causes a person to run, and running produces fear.

*This is the **conclusion** of a chapter on emotion, stress, and coping.*

Summary

Emotion

1. Emotion, or affect, is an evaluative response (a positive or negative feeling state) that typically includes subjective experience, physiological arousal, and behavioral expression.

2. The **James-Lange theory** asserts that the subjective experience of emotion results from bodily experience induced by an emotion-eliciting stimulus. According to this theory, we do not run because we are afraid; we become afraid because we run (and our hearts pound). In contrast, the **Cannon-Bard theory** proposes that emotion-inducing stimuli simultaneously elicit both emotional experience and bodily responses. Although both theories have their strengths and limitations, recent research suggests that different emotions are, as James believed, associated with distinct, innate patterns of autonomic nervous system arousal.

3. **Emotional expression** refers to facial and other outward indications of emotion, such as body language and tone of voice. Many aspects of emotional expression, particularly facial expression, are innate and cross-culturally universal. Culturally variable patterns of regulating and displaying emotion are called **display rules.**

4. Psychologists have attempted to produce a list of **basic emotions,** emotions common to the human species from which all other emotions and emotional blends can be derived. Anger, fear, happiness, sadness, and disgust are listed by all theorists as basic. An even more fundamental distinction is between **positive affect** and **negative affect,** which is related, as well, to approach-oriented versus avoidance-oriented motives.

5. Emotions are controlled by neural pathways distributed throughout the nervous system. The hypothalamus activates sympathetic and endocrine responses related to emotion. The limbic system, and particularly the amygdala, is part of an emotional circuit that includes the hypothalamus. The amygdala is the brain's "emotional computer" for calculating the affective significance of a stimulus. The cortex plays several roles with respect to emotion, particularly in the appraisal of events.

6. The behaviorist perspective on emotion points to approach and avoidance systems associated with positive and negative affect, respectively. According to the psychodynamic perspective, people can be unconscious of their own emotional experience, which can nonetheless influence thought, behavior, and even health.

7. From a cognitive perspective, the way people respond emotionally depends on the **attributions** they make—that is, their inferences about causes of the emotion and their own bodily sensations. According to the **Schachter-Singer theory,** emotion involves -two factors: physiological arousal and cognitive interpretation of the arousal. Emotion and **mood** (relatively extended emotional states which, unlike emotions, typically do not disrupt ongoing activities) have an impact on encoding, retrieval, judgment, and decision making.

8. The evolutionary perspective on emotion derives from Charles Darwin's view that emotions serve an adaptive purpose. Emotion has both communicative and motivational functions.

9. Stress

10. **Stress** refers to a challenge to a person's capacity to adapt to inner and outer demands, which may be physiologically arousing and emotionally taxing and call for cognitive and behavioral responses. Stress is a psychobiological process that entails a transaction between a person and her environment. Selye proposed that the body responds to stressful conditions with a **general adaptation syndrome** consisting of three stages: alarm, resistance, and exhaustion.

11. From a psychological standpoint, stress entails a person's perception that demands of the environment tax or exceed his available psychosocial resources. Stress, in this view, depends on the meaning of an event to the individual. Lazarus's model identifies two stages in the process of stress and coping: **primary appraisal**, in which the person decides whether the situation is benign, stressful, or irrelevant; and secondary appraisal, in which the person evaluates the options and decides how to respond.

12. Events that often lead to stress are called stressors. **Stressors** include life events, catastrophes, and daily hassles.

13. Stress has a considerable impact on health and mortality, particularly through its effects on the immune system. Whether a person under stress re-mains healthy or becomes ill also depends in part on the person's enduring personality dispositions. **Type A behavior pattern**, and particularly its hostility component, has been linked to heart disease. Neuroticism (tendency to experience negative affective states), power motivation, hardiness, and optimism/pessimism are other personality traits linked to stress and health.

Coping

1. People cope by trying to change the situation directly, changing their perception of it, or changing the emotions it engenders. The ways people deal with stressful situations are known as strategies for **coping**; coping mechanisms are in part culturally patterned.

2. A major resource for coping with stress is **social support**, which is related to health and longevity.

Your Text

Try this strategy on a chapter from your own textbook that you need to read this week. Fill in both columns.

> The introduction and conclusion strategy is a 'during the reading' strategy. You write the ideas as you read. It can also be used as an 'after the reading strategy'. You review your notes after you read the chapter and when you wish to study from it.

CHAPTER: **PAGES:**

Main Topics

List the main topics in the introduction and conclusion

Supporting Details

Fill in details as you read the chapter section by section

_____
_____
_____
_____
_____
_____
_____
_____
_____
_____
_____
_____
_____
_____
_____
_____
_____
_____
_____
_____
_____
_____
_____
_____
_____
_____
_____
_____
_____
_____
_____
_____
_____
_____

Strategy Feedback Prompt

This exercise is meant to be reflective in nature as you consider how you liked the strategy. Finish completing the prompt after you apply the strategy to your content area textbook.

Learning to think about what works for you is important as you take command of your learning.

Module #:
Module Name:

Describe how to do the strategy in detail:

Chapter title and number worked on today:

Outcome: Write a paragraph about your use of the strategy with your own textbook. Comment on the following and add any other thoughts that you would like to share: *How well did the strategy work on your own textbook chapter? Did you have to adjust the strategy when applying it to your own textbook chapter? How? What did you get out of this module?*

Mastery Assessment

The Mastery Assessment for this module involves making and answering probable test questions based on the work you completed in your practice.

> You will need to assess your learning in order to discover your strengths and weaknesses.

Introduction/Conclusion Breakdown

Make up probable test questions based on your practice assignment. Answer your questions.

1.

2.

3.

4.

5.

6.

7.

8.

9.

10.

11.

12.

13.

14.

15.

Module 15

Power Point Slides

Introduction

The purpose of this module is to promote your use of the slides provided by your teacher, and/or to encourage you to create slides if none are provided. Slides are a great resource to help you understand your text. They are mini summaries of all of the significant information. In an attempt to help you understand the text, your teacher may have made power point slides of this important information. These slides are a result of determining the main ideas and then the supporting detail. If you have never made slides of your own, it is a great strategy that forces you to understand the text and break down the material into a more manageable study guide.

> Using slides that have been created by your professor is an excellent way to get the most out of the chapter as you read.

Step-by-Step Strategy Description

Choose A or B

A) Slides created by professor.

1. Choose a chapter and print out the power point slides provided by your professor.
2. On each slide, place a page number where the information can be located in the text.
3. Read the correlating text page.
4. Add comments of clarification and/or any additional information to help you remember/understand the concepts. Use your own words, do not copy directly from the text.
5. Add a blank slide somewhere.
6. Be prepared to show your slides to the class. You will talk through your slides. When you get to the blank slide, you will continue to talk about the content of the chapter to show that you know what you are talking about.

OR

B) Slides created by you.

1. Choose a chapter and complete a preview.
2. Read and highlight the chapter, section by section.
3. Create slides based on your highlighted information. This is very similar to making margin notes except you are creating your notes on a visual slide show.
4. Add an introductory slide and a concluding slide.
5. Add a blank slide somewhere.
6. Be prepared to show your slides to the class. You will talk through your slides. When you get to the blank slide, you will continue to talk about the content of the chapter to show proof that you know what you are talking about.

Using the sample readings that follow, try this strategy on the practice textbook excerpt.
When you finish, compare your slide to your classmates' slides.

Creating your own slides is a 'during the reading' activity. Using slides that have been created by your professor is also a 'during the reading' activity.

Make one practice slide here:

Topic: _____

Details:

Sample Reading for Module 15

Some theorists suggest that humans have a related motive to know and understand the world around them (Epstein, 1990). Pleasure in knowing and displeasure in feeling uncertain may have evolved as mechanisms that foster exploration of the environment. Another self-oriented motive is self-esteem. Theorists of many theoretical persuasions—psychodynamic (Kohut, 1971), humanistic (Rogers, 1959), and cognitive-social (Higgins, 1990), among others—view self-esteem motivation—the need to view oneself in a positive light—as a fundamental motivator of behavior [...].

Need for Achievement

The **need for achievement**—to do well, to succeed, and to avoid failure—is the best researched psychosocial motive. This is not surprising in view of our own culture's emphasis on personal achievement in school, sports, careers, and practically every domain in which our actions can be described in terms of success and failure. In general, people high in achievement motivation tend to choose moderately difficult tasks (those with about a 50/50 chance of success) over very easy or very difficult tasks (Atkinson, 1977; Slade & Rush, 1991). They enjoy being challenged and take pleasure in accomplishing a difficult task but are often motivated to avoid failure. In one study, subjects played a ring-toss game and were free to choose their own distance from the target (Atkinson & Litwin, 1960). Those who scored high in achievement motivation selected distances that were challenging but not impossible. In contrast, subjects who scored low in achievement motivation and had a high fear of failure stood either very close to the target or impossibly far, which guaranteed either success or a good excuse for failing.

How do experimental findings such as these translate into everyday behaviors? People with a high need for achievement tend to work more persistently than others to achieve a goal, and they take more pride in their accomplishments when they succeed (Atkinson, 1977). Not surprisingly, they are consequently more likely to succeed. They also tend to attribute their past successes to their abilities and their past failures to forces beyond their control, which increases confidence and persistence in the face of adverse feedback (Dweck, 1975; Meece et al, 1990; Weiner, 1974). A student with high achievement motivation is likely to select a major that suits his abilities, commit to a study schedule that is rigorous but not impossible, and work hard to succeed within those limits.

The consequences of achievement motivation extend far beyond the classroom or the laboratory. In an economically depressed area of India, where government programs had been ineffective in raising the standard of living, psychologist David McClelland undertook an interesting experiment. He taught local businessmen to fantasize about high achievement and to problem-solve ways to succeed (McClelland, 1978; McClelland & Winter, 1969). Over time, they began new businesses and employed new workers at a much higher rate than businessmen in a comparable town in the same region. In Western cultures, achievement motivation also predicts occupational success, such as how well a car salesperson can move cars off the lot (Barling et al., 1996).

Components of Achievement Motivation

As with other motives, people do not express achievement in every domain. For example, the achievement-oriented science student may place little value in succeeding in philosophy courses or may be undisturbed by her failure to bake a tasty soufflé. From a cognitive perspective, motives may be expressed selectively because they are hierarchically organized, with some sections of the hierarchy carrying more motivational weight than others (Figure 10.10).

Achievement goals themselves appear to reflect a blend of at least three motives (Elliott & Church, 1997; Elliott & Harackiewicz, 1996). When people set a goal—doing well in a class, becoming a scientist, or running a marathon—they may be motivated by the desire to meet a socially defined standard (such as a good grade), to avoid failure, or to master the skill. These are called performance-approach, performance-avoidance, and mastery goals.,

Performance goals are motives to achieve at a particular level, usually one that meets a socially defined standard, such as getting an A in a class (Dweck, 1986). The emphasis of performance goals is on the *outcome,* that is, on success or failure in meeting a standard. Some people are more motivated to *attain* a goal, whereas others are more motivated by the fear of not attaining it. When performance goals center on approaching or attaining a standard, they are called **performance-approach goals.** If I am spending a weekend skiing, for example, I may be motivated by the desire to say I skied a black-diamond slope—a slope of considerable difficulty. When performance goals center less on achieving a high standard than on avoiding failure, particularly publicly observable failure, they are called **performance-avoidance goals.** I may, for example, stay on the baby slopes to avoid skiing down the hill on my buttocks.

Performance goals, whether for approach or avoidance, are about achieving a concrete outcome—obtaining success or avoiding failure. In contrast, mastery goals are motives to increase one's competence, mastery, or skill. If I am motivated by mastery goals, my interest is in developing my skill or technique—enjoying the sheer pleasure of skiing more quickly or competently—not in being able to brag about my exploits on the slopes or avoid the snickers of even little children passing by. (My own goals in skiing are probably now apparent.)

Parenting, Culture, and Achievement

The need for achievement is primarily a learned motive, which numerous studies have linked to patterns of childrearing. Children with high achievement motivation tend to have parents who encourage them to attempt new tasks slightly beyond their reach, praise success when it occurs, encourage independent thinking, discourage complaining, and prompt their children to try

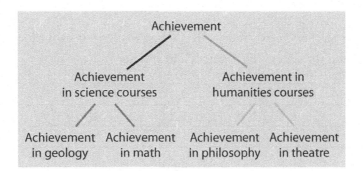

Figure 10.10 Cognitive structure of achievement motivation. A student in the sciences attaches different motivational weights to different sections of the hierarchy. Dark lines indicate strong motivation; light lines indicate weaker motivation.

new solutions when they fail (McClelland, 1985; Weiss & Schwarz, 1996; Winterbottom, 1953).

Parenting always occurs within a cultural context, and motivation for achievement varies considerably across cultures and historical periods. McClelland and his colleagues (1953) have explored some of the links among culture, childrearing, and achievement. In several studies, they rated the extent of achievement imagery in stories and folktales, particularly those told to children.

> Power point slides are very useful to study from as you prepare for tests. Creating your own slides is a 'during the reading' activity. Adding information to your professor's slides is also a 'during the reading' activity. Using the slides that have been created by you or your professor is an 'after the reading' activity.

Your Text

Try this strategy on a chapter from your content area class that you need to read this week.

CHAPTER: **PAGES:**

Did you use your teacher created slides OR did you make your own slides? Please describe in detail how you used the slides. What exactly did you do?

_____
_____
_____
_____
_____
_____
_____
_____
_____
_____

What is the advantage of using your teacher's created slides?

_____
_____
_____
_____
_____
_____
_____
_____
_____
_____
_____

What is the advantage of creating your own slides?

_____
_____
_____
_____
_____
_____
_____
_____
_____
_____

Strategy Feedback Prompt:

> Learning to think about what works for you is important as you take command of your learning.

This exercise is meant to be reflective in nature as you consider how you liked the strategy. Finish completing the prompt after you apply the strategy to your content area textbook.

Module #:
Module Name:

Describe how to do the strategy in detail:

Chapter title and number worked on today:

Outcome: Write a paragraph about your use of the strategy with your own textbook. Comment on the following and add any other thoughts that you would like to share: *How well did the strategy work on your own textbook chapter? Did you have to adjust the strategy when applying it to your own textbook chapter? How? What did you get out of this module?*

Mastery Assessment

You will present your slides and hand in your printed slides as the Mastery Assessment.

Module 16

Test Construction

Introduction

One of the easiest ways to ensure that you are paying attention when you read a text is to be accountable for the information you have just read. You can do this by making up simple questions that relate to the reading for EACH page of the reading.

> Constructing test questions from the reading helps you think deeply about the content of the reading.

Step-by-Step Strategy Description

1. Choose a chapter or a section of a chapter for focus.
2. Read and highlight the first page.
3. Create 3 questions based on the information. (multiple choice, fill in the blank, or any short answer)
4. Read the next page and create another 3 questions based on the information.
5. Continue in this manner until you have completed the chapter or section. (3 questions per page)
6. Make a blank test and a separate answer key.

> Learning to test yourself requires many opportunities for practice in thinking through problems and issues and in applying concepts.

Your Text

Try this strategy on a practice textbook excerpt. When you finish, check your work against the text.

CHAPTER: **PAGES:**

> Test Construction is an 'after the reading' activity. You make up your test questions after you have read the chapter and used other strategies to help you get through the reading.

Strategy Feedback Prompt

This exercise is meant to be reflective in nature as you consider how you liked the strategy. Finish completing the prompt after you apply the strategy to your content area textbook.

> Learning to think about what works for you is important as you take command of your learning.

Module #:

Module Name:

Describe how to do the strategy in detail:

Chapter title and number worked on today:

Outcome: Write a paragraph about your use of the strategy with your own textbook. Comment on the following and add any other thoughts that you would like to share: *How well did the strategy work on your own textbook chapter? Did you have to adjust the strategy when applying it to your own textbook chapter? How? What did you get out of this module?*

Mastery Assessment

The Mastery Assessment for this module involves taking the test you created.

> You will need to assess your learning in order to discover your strengths and weaknesses.

Take the test that you made!

Website Resources

There are many websites that are fun and that can help you study. Check out any site that is a study tool and apply what you know:

http://quizlet.com – quizzes, flashcards, games, and more.
http://www.lessonpaths.com – create and share learning playlists
http://www.humanline.com/en/ – visual library
http://www.3dtoad.com/ – interactive 3D images

Find three additional resources that would be useful to use for studying in your discipline.

Module 17

Summarizing

Introduction

Each chapter in your textbook will most likely have some sort of summary. The entire chapter is condensed into a few paragraphs in order to present the significant information. The purpose of this module is to encourage you to distinguish between the main ideas and the details and then write a summary of the material.

> The primary headings, subheadings, and subcategories can function as an outline for summarizing the entire section or chapter.

A summary begins with a clear, concise thesis statement of the reading. The thesis statement effectively expresses what the entire chapter or section is about in one sentence. The rest of the summary includes statements from each section of the chapter or each subsection within a major heading.

Step-by-Step Strategy Description

1. Choose a chapter for focus.
2. Read and highlight the chapter or a section of the chapter.
3. Using the title of the chapter or section, write a thesis statement.
4. Using the first heading, write a sentence that summarizes what that section is about.
5. Continue with the next heading and so on until you have finished the chapter or section.
6. Remember to use your own words as you write your summary in paragraph format.

> Using your own words as you write a summary of a section or an entire chapter helps you gain a broad understanding of the reading.

Using the sample reading that follows, try this strategy on the practice textbook excerpt.
When you finish, you can check your work against the text.

> Summarizing is a 'during the reading' activity. As you read each headed section, you write a sentence that summarizes what you have just read.

Thesis statement for entire chapter or section:

This chapter examines the psychodynamic, cognitive, biological, and alternative views on dreaming and elaborates on the types of sleep disorders.

Using a paragraph format, for EACH heading and/or subheading, write a sentence summarizing what the section is about.

Sample Reading for Module 17

Sleep and Dreaming

After a period of REM sleep, the person descends again through Stage 2 and on to delta sleep. A complete cycle of REM and NREM sleep occurs about every 90 minutes (Figure 9.12). However, as the night progresses, the person spends less of the 90 minutes in delta sleep and more in REM sleep. Rapid eye movement sleep recurs four or five times a night and accounts for about 25 percent of all time asleep (on the average, two hours per night). Thus, over the course of a lifetime, the average person spends an estimated 50,000 hours—2000 days, or six full years—dreaming (Hobson, 1988).

INTERIM SUMMARY: Sleep proceeds through a series of stages that can be assessed by EEC The major distinction is between **rapid eye movement** (REM) and **non-REM** (NREM) **sleep.** Most dreaming occurs in REM sleep, in which the eyes dart around and the EEG takes on an active pattern resembling waking consciousness. Perception of external stimuli and the capacity to move are substantially curtailed during REM sleep.

Three Views of Dreaming

For thousands of years, humans have speculated about the nature and significance of dreams. Some cultures view dreams as actions carried out by the dreamer's soul. Others regard dreams as indices of the dreamer's deepest desires, revelations from the spiritual world, or sources of supernatural power (Bourguignon, 1979).

In the West in the late nineteenth century, dream interpretation was considered the realm of "primitives" and charlatans. Freud, however, argued that dream interpretation is a legitimate scientific and psychological pursuit. Versions of his psychodynamic theory are among the major approaches to dreaming. The other approaches are cognitive and biological.

A Psychodynamic View

Freud (1900) believed that dreams, like all mental events, have meaning but must be deciphered by someone skilled in dream interpretation. As communications spoken in the language of the unconscious, which is irrational and wishful, dreams are often vague, illogical, or bizarre and thus require translation into the language of rational waking consciousness. For example, in dreams two people are often condensed into one, or thoughts about one person are displaced

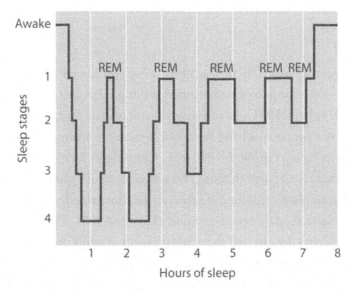

Figure 9.12 REM sleep. The stages of sleep follow a cyclical pattern that occurs about every 90 minutes, from Stage 1 through delta sleep and back again. As the night progresses, the person spends less time in deeper sleep and more time in REM sleep. Source: Cartwright, 1978.

onto someone else (that is, ascribed to the wrong person). According to Freud, unconscious processes are associative processes; thus, ideas are connected by their relationship to one another along networks of association, not by logic. During sleep, a person is not using conscious, rational processes to create or monitor the story so one thought or image can easily be activated in place of another.

In this sense, Freud saw dreams as "the insanity of the night," where associative thinking replaces logical thought. For example, a man who was angry at his father had a dream of murdering his father's best friend, presumably because anger and murder were associatively linked, as were his father and his father's friend. According to Freud, people often rapidly forget their dreams upon awakening because dreams contain elements of unconscious mental life that would be anxiety provoking and are repressed during normal waking consciousness.

Freud distinguished between the **manifest content**, or story line of the dream and the **latent content**, of its underlying meaning. He proposed that the underlying meaning of every dream is an unconscious wish, typically a forbidden sexual of aggressive desire. The empirical data do not support this hypothesis (see Fisher & Greenberg, 1997), and today, most psychodynamic psychologists believe, rather, that the latent content can be a wish, a fear or anything else that is emotionally pressing. To uncover the content of a dream, the dreamer free associates to each part of the dreams (that is, simply says aloud whatever thoughts come to mind about it), while the dream analyst tries to trace the networks of association involved in the dream's construction. Probably the most central aspect of the psychodynamic approach is its view of dreams as *associative thought* laden with *emotional concerns*.

A Cognitive View

A cognitive perspective suggests; that dreams are cognitive constructions that reflect the concerns and metaphors people express in their waking thought (Antrobus, 1991; Domhoff, 1996; Foulkes, 1978; Hall, 1951). In the view, dreams are simply a form of thought. At times, they may even serve a problem-solving function, presenting dreamers with potential solutions to problems they are facing during the day (e.g., Cartwright, 1996). Dreams rely on the same metaphors people use in everyday thinking; however, conscious monitoring is deactivated during dreaming, so metaphoric thinking is relatively unconstrained, leading to images or events that may seem bizarre to the conscious mind (Lakoff, 1997). Dreams also show cognitive development: Children's dreams lack the sophistication of adult dreams (Foulkes, 1982).

A Grammar of Dreams One cognitive viewpoint that shares many points with Freud's theory was proposed by dream researcher David Foulkes (Cavallero & Foulkes, 1993; Foulkes, 1978, 1995). Like many contemporary psychodynamic psychologists, Foulkes takes issue with the contention that the latent meaning of every dream is an unconscious wish. He proposes instead that dreams simply express current concerns of one sort or another in a language with its own peculiar grammar. The manifest content is constructed from the latent content through rules of transformation, that is, rules for putting a thought or concern into the "language" of dreaming.

Decoding dream language thus requires a knowledge of those rules of transformation, just as a transformational grammar allows linguists to transform surface structure into deep structure [...]. In everyday language, the sentence "The boy threw the ball" can be transformed into "The ball was thrown by the boy" In dream language, the thought "I am worried about my upcoming exam" can be translated into a dream about falling off a cliff.

Dreams and Current Concerns Evidence that dreams are related to current concerns—whether wishes, fears, or preoccupations of other sorts—comes not only from the clinic but also from empirical research (Domhoff, 1996). A study of dreams of Israeli medical students five weeks into the Gulf War, when Saddam Hussein was threatening Israel with Scud missile attacks, found that over half the dream reports of students dealt with themes of war or attack (Lavie, 1996). Other research finds that the extent to which people's dreams express wishes for intimacy correlates with their desires for intimacy by day (Evans & Singer, 1994).

Gender and cross-cultural differences also support the view that dreams express concerns similar to those that people experience in their waking consciousness (Domhoff, 1996). Just as males tend to be more aggressive than females by day, their dreams show a greater ratio of aggressive to friendly interactions than do women's dreams. Similarly, the Netherlands and Switzerland are two of the least violent technologically developed societies, whereas the United States is the most violent. Strikingly, incidents involving physical aggression are about 20 percent more prevalent in the dreams of U.S. males and females than among their Dutch and Swiss counterparts.

Although the evidence is sketchy and inconsistent, some research suggests that dreams may not only reflect but even influence conscious experience and concerns. For example, one study compared dream reports in migraine headache sufferers before and after the day of a migraine attack (Heather-Greener et al., 1996). Strikingly; pre-migraine dreams were characterized by a greater incidence of anger, aggressive interactions, themes of misfortune, and apprehension. Whether these worries revealed at night played a role in *causing* the headaches or simply provided an index of an impending migraine attack is unclear. In another study, women undergoing divorce who dreamed more about their ex-spouse and had more dream interactions depicting efforts to deal with and get over the divorce were less depressed a year later (Cartwright, 1996). Again, whether the dream served a problem-solving function or simply reflected the progress of the women's grieving is unknown.

A Biological View

Some dream researchers argue that dreams are biological phenomena with no meaning at all. (e.g., Crick & Mitchison, 1983). According, to one such theory (Hobson, 1988; Hobson & McCarley, 1977), dreams reflect cortical interpretations of random neural signals initiated in the midbrain during REM sleep. These signals are relayed through the thalamus to the visual and association cortex, which tries to understand this information in its usual way, namely, by using existing knowledge structures (schemas) to process the information. Because the initial signals are essentially random, however, the interpretations proposed by the cortex rarely make logical sense. Many dream researchers have, however, criticized this view, arguing that the presence of dreams during NREM sleep and the absence of any clear evidence linking specific patterns of midbrain activation with specific patterns of dream content suggest that it is at least incomplete (Foulkes, 1995; Squier & Domhoff, 1997).

> *You would wish to be responsible for everything except your dreams! What miserable weakness, what lack of logical courage! Nothing contains more of your own work than your dreams! Nothing belongs to you so much! Substance, form, duration, actor, spectator—in these comedies you act as your complete selves!*
>
> **Nietzsche,**
> *Thus Spake Zarathustra*

Integrating the Alternative Models

Are these three models of dreaming really incompatible? The psychodynamic and cognitive views converge on the notion that dreams express current ideas and concerns in a highly symbolic language that requires decoding. They differ over the extent to which those concerns involve deep-seated or repressed wishes and fears. In reality dreams probably express motives (wishes and fears) as well as ideas. Many motives have cognitive components, such as representations of wished-for or feared states [...]. Thus, a fear of failing an examination includes a representation of the feared scenario and its possible consequences. What applies to cognition, then, probably applies to many aspects of motivation as well, so dreams are as likely to express motives as beliefs.

Moreover, the biological explanation of dreaming is not necessarily incompatible with either the psychodynamic or the cognitive view. The interpretive processes that occur at the cortical level involve the same structures of meaning—schemas, associational networks, and emotional processes—posited by Freud and Foulkes. Hence, even random activation of these structures would produce dreams that reveal something about the organisation of thoughts and feelings in the person's mind, particularly those that have received chronic or recent activation.

INTERIM SUMMARY: Freud viewed dreams as a window to the language of unconscious associative thoughts, feelings, and wishes. He distinguished the **latent content,** or underlying meaning, from the **manifest content,** or story line. Although Freud believed that the latent content of every dream is an unconscious wish that has been repressed, empirical data do not support this view, and most psychodynamic theorists and clinicians instead believe that the latent content can be a wish, a fear, or anything else that is emotionally pressing. The cognitive perspective suggests that dreams are the outcome of cognitive processes and that their content reflects the concerns and metaphors people express in their waking cognition. A biological view of dreaming proposes that dreams reflect cortical interpretations of random neural signals arising from the midbrain during REM sleep. These three views are probably not incompatible.

Sleep Disorders

Most people have experienced occasional bouts of **insomnia** (inability to sleep) tossing and turning from anxiety or excitement. More enduring sleep disturbances, or **sleep disorders,** result from, a number of biological and psychosocial causes (see Rothenberg, 1997). Insomnia and **hypersomnia** (sleeping too much) are frequent symptoms of depression, since the neurotransmitter systems that mediate mood are also involved in the regulation of circadian rhythms. Anxiety and depression can also impair sleep even when the causes are not primarily biological (see Ware, 1997). Trauma survivors show an elevated incidence of sleep disorders, including nightmares and insomnia (Ross et al., 1989; Yehuda & McFarlane, 1997). Following the massive earthquake that struck San Francisco in 1989, the incidence of nightmares in general, as well as nightmares about earthquakes in particular, rose dramatically (Wood et al., 1992).

Sleep disturbances may persist for years, even decades, after a traumatic experience, particularly if the trauma was prolonged. Survivors of the Nazi Holocaust, now primarily in their sixties and seventies, continue to have significantly more sleep disturbances than comparison subjects—over five decades after the experience (Rosen et al., 1991). The longer subjects spent in the camps, the more sleep disturbance they currently report.

No single treatment is effective for all patients with sleep disorders. Some respond better to psychological treatments, others to biological treatments (such as medications), and others to combination therapies (Buysee et al., 1995). "Sleeping pills," however, should always be taken with caution, since they can have paradoxical effects: They can sometimes lead to more, rather than less, trouble sleeping, as the person becomes dependent on them or the brain develops a tolerance for them, requiring higher doses to achieve the same effect (Lavie, 1996).

Insomnia

The most common sleep disorder is insomnia, which may take one of several forms: initial insomnia (difficulty falling asleep), middle insomnia (typically, frequent awakenings during the night), and early morning insomnia (waking up consistently around four o'clock and being unable to return to sleep) (Reynolds et al., 1991). As prevalent as insomnia is, researchers often find a substantial discrepancy between patients' self-reports of insomnia and their actual sleep patterns when assessed in the laboratory. People who claim to have severe insomnia frequently do sleep several hours, but they think they have not slept at all.

Insomnia often results from stress, but it can become a source of stress as well if it becomes chronic (Rosch, 1996). Insomnia can create a vicious cycle, in which the insomniac starts to worry that she will not be able to sleep as soon as she gets into bed. Essentially, the bed becomes a conditioned stimulus that elicits anxiety, which in turn fuels the insomnia. Sleeping pills can exacerbate the sleep disturbance by interfering with natural sleep processes (Hindmarch, 1991). A better strategy is to establish a regular bedtime, avoid activities that activate the sympathetic nervous system before bedtime (such as exercising or drinking beverages containing caffeine), and get up rather than roll around restlessly in bed (Bootzin et al., 1991). Table 9.1 lists some suggestions by a major sleep researcher for reducing or avoiding insomnia.

TABLE **9.1 Suggestions for Avoiding or Reducing Insomnia**
1. Avoid spending too much time in bed. If you are awake, get out. Do not let the bed become a conditioned stimulus associated with insomnia and anxiety.
2. Do not try to force sleep. Go to bed when you are ready, and get out if you are not.
3. Do not keep a brightly lit, ticking clock near the bed.
4. Avoid physical activity late at night. It activates the autonomic nervous system, which is incompatible with sleep.
5. Avoid coffee, chocolate, or alcohol before bedtime. Caffeine will keep you up, even if you do not think it affects you, and alcohol often causes people to wake up in the middle of the night.
6. Keep a regular sleep schedule. If you have insomnia, you need more of a routine than most people.
7. Do not eat a large meal before bedtime. If you wake up, do not visit the refrigerator.
8. Avoid sleeping during the day if you have insomnia.
Source: Adapted from P. Lavie, *The Enchanted World of Sleep* (A. Berris, Trans.), Yale University Press, New Haven, CT, 1996, pp. 176–177.

Nightmares, Night Terrors, Sleep Apnea, and Narcolepsy

Other sleep disorders include nightmares, night terrors, sleep apnea, and narcolepsy. Nightmares are vivid, frightening dreams typically associated with fears like falling, death, or calamity (see Bearden, 1994). About 5 percent of the general population suffers from chronic nightmares (Bixler et al., 1979); not surprisingly, sufferers of chronic nightmares tend to have other emotional problems or histories of trauma (Berquier & Ashton, 1992). Nightmares typically occur during REM sleep and thus can take place at any time during the night. In contrast, night terrors—dramatic experiences of intense terror or panic during sleep—typically occur during delta sleep and hence tend to take place in the first two or three hours of sleep. Unlike nightmares, which people usually vividly recall, individuals seldom remember the contents of night terrors upon wakening. Instead, they may scream and awaken, feeling very confused.

Another disorder is **sleep apnea,** which usually produces symptoms of chronic sleepiness because the person is awakened as many as several hundred times during the night. In sleep apnea, breathing typically stops for more than ten seconds at a time, leaving the person gasping for air. People with sleep apnea often do not know the cause of their distress; they are aware only of feeling as if they have not slept. Their bed partners, however, may be quite aware of their loud snoring and restless sleep. Sleep apnea typically occurs in overweight men.

Narcolepsy is a sleep disorder of the day rather than the night. Narcoleptics are subject to sudden sleep attacks, falling into REM sleep in the middle of talking, driving, laughing, or other, activities. Narcolepsy is often genetically transmitted, although the incidence varies cross-culturally In Japan, one in 600 people suffers from the disorder, whereas in North America the prevalence is more on the order of one in 10,000 (Aldrich, 1990). Narcoleptics often find themselves continuously battling the urge to sleep and hence experience a constant state of fatigue and sleepiness. As with some of the other sleep disorders, medications can often be useful in controlling the symptoms of narcolepsy, although a cure has not been developed (see Buysse et al., 1995).

Your Text

Try this strategy on a chapter from your content area class that you need to read this week.

CHAPTER: **PAGES:**

> The thought process of summarizing is very similar to margin notes. To help you write a coherent paragraph you can add transitions.

Thesis statement for entire chapter or section:

Using a paragraph format write a sentence summarizing what EACH section (heading and/or subheading) is about.

Strategy Feedback Prompt

This exercise is meant to be reflective in nature as you consider how you liked the strategy. Finish completing the prompt **after** you apply the strategy to your content area textbook.

> Learning to think about what works for you is important as you take command of your learning.

Module #:
Module Name:

Describe how to do the strategy in detail:

Chapter title and number worked on today:

Outcome: Write a paragraph about your use of the strategy with your own textbook. Comment on the following and add any other thoughts that you would like to share: *How well did the strategy work on your own textbook chapter? Did you have to adjust the strategy when applying it to your own textbook chapter? How? What did you get out of this module?*

Module 18

Strategy Application

Introduction

The purpose of this module is to promote thinking and learning across the curriculum. You will find that every course's curriculum is different, every text has its level of difficulty, and every teacher has a different style of teaching. This module presents a variety of scenarios that you may encounter as a student. It encourages thought as you decide how to proceed.

> Using a positive attitude while reading encourages success.

Step-by-Step Strategy Description:

1. Read each scenario.
2. Describe your approach if you were taking this class.
3. Write a detailed description on how you would proceed
   a) In class strategy
   b) Outside of class strategy
   c) With the textbook strategy – identify pre-reading, during the reading, or after the reading strategy

Defend your answer.

> Making goals helps you stay on the path to successful reading across content areas.

Strategy Application
Scenario 1
You are enrolled in an American History class. When you arrive on the first day of class, you discover that you know no one else in the class. The class is taught in a large auditorium and there are about 200 students there. Each class is 50 minutes long and the professor stands in the front of the auditorium and lectures the entire time. There is no class discussion and only a few visuals that are used during the lecture. There is a textbook that is a typical history book – large, heavy and full of print with few pictures.

How would you proceed? Describe and explain below.

In class strategy application

Outside of class application

Textbook strategy application

Strategy defense

Strategy Application
Scenario 2

You are enrolled in a sociology course with about 30 other students. The professor uses power point slides during each lecture. In addition, there is a lot of opportunity for discussion in class. During the third week of the course, the professor cancels class due to illness. The class does not meet for 3 more sessions due to the professor's illness. The midterm is scheduled for the 5th week of the quarter and you have not met for 2 weeks. You receive an e-mail from the professor that the schedule will not be altered and the midterm is still on schedule. You will be responsible for knowing the first 5 chapters in the book and power point slides have been posted on blackboard for these chapters. There is no study guide posted.

How would you proceed? Describe and explain below.

In class strategy application

Outside of class application

Textbook strategy application

Strategy defense

Strategy Application
Scenario 3

You are preparing for an exam in psychology. The exam will cover about 8 chapters from your course textbook and your class notes. The test is in two weeks. The text focuses primarily on concepts and vocabulary from those chapters. You have been told that the test will include application-type questions in which you are expected to choose the appropriate term that illustrates the concept. What would be the best reading/study strategies?

How would you proceed? Describe and explain below.

In class strategy application

Outside of class application

Textbook strategy application

Strategy defense

Strategy Application
Scenario 4

Create your own scenario based on the courses that you are currently participating in. Refer to Scenarios 1, 2, and 3 to help you make up your own.

Strategy Feedback Prompt

This exercise is meant to be reflective in nature as you consider what you learned.

> Learning to think about what works for you is important as you take command of your learning.

Module #:

Module Name:

Describe how this strategy was useful to you. What did you get out of this module?

Module 19

Metacognition and Personal Application

Introduction

The purpose of this module is to encourage you to process how these strategies have affected your behaviors, grades, motivation, thinking and your reading process. Each question emphasizes metacognition—thinking about thinking. There are four parts to this module. In the first part, you will watch a podcast video; in the second part, you will answer the reflective questions; in the third part, you will prepare a presentation for the class; and in the fourth part, you will answer questions about class participation in your content class for one day.

> Embracing your role as a student will help you meet the milestones before you.

Step-by-Step Strategy Description

> To solve problems effectively, you need to know how your mind works and how you perform cognitive tasks such as remembering, learning, and problem solving.

Metacognition and Personal Application

I. **Go to You Tube and type in the word metacognition. Watch the videos and podcasts on metacognition. List the video/podcasts here that you liked best.**

Thinking about how you think will help you become a better student. I. Watch the podcast video. II. Answer the questions. III. Prepare something to teach from your textbook.

II. Answer the questions that follow.

1. What are goals for studying?

2. What is characteristic of learning? (How do you know when you have actually learned something?)

3. What are strategies?

4. Describe a strategy to use BEFORE reading the textbook.

5. Describe a strategy to use WHILE reading the textbook.

6. Describe a strategy to use AFTER reading the textbook.

7. Do the textbook strategies that you are now learning affect your confidence? If so how?

8. Do the textbook strategies that you are now learning affect your motivation? If so, how?

9. Prior to this quarter, how would you have described yourself as a student?

10. Has your description of yourself changed? If so, how?

11. Tell one thing that you would like to change about yourself as a student?

12. Which textbook strategy that you have learned has worked the best for you? <u>Why?</u>

13. Which textbook strategy that you have learned has been the least helpful? <u>Why?</u>

14. Identify one goal that you would like to work on using textbook strategies.

15. Tell how you plan to achieve that goal.

III. **Prepare to teach the class some concept, idea, or section of your textbook. You must use a visual aid.**

> Modeling appropriate academic behaviors promotes both learning the strategy AND learning the content.

The best way to prove that you have learned something is to have to teach it to someone else. Choose something from your declared text that you do not know but need to know for a test. Study the information and be prepared to teach it to your classmates. You will present a 5-10 minute lesson on this idea or concept. You need a visual aid in the form of a poster, handout, object, or anything else that is sufficient for a visual representation to keep audience interest.

Chapter Title and #:_____

Selected Topic_____

Point breakdown:
  Visual aid _____
  Knowledge of concept or idea _____
  Presentation _____
  Total points _____

IV. **Metacognitive Exercise - reflection on content class participation**

Consider one specific time that you attended your content class. Answer the following questions based on your experience during the entire lesson.

Identify course _____   Date and time of experience _____

1. Seat location:
    How difficult was it for you to interact with the other students based on your seat location?
    How difficult was it for you to interact with the professor based on your seat location?
    Do you believe that students who sit in the front of the classroom are more successful in their interactions in a class?
2. Attentiveness
    Did any private conversation or person distract you during the lesson?
    How would you feel if your professor separated you from other students who may distract you during the lesson?
3. Participation
    Did you more frequently raise your hand or just talk out when participating in class?
    Do you prefer to just talk out when you wish to participate or do prefer a class where you are required to raise your hand?
    Which way do you feel most valued?

4. Concentration

Did your cell phone distract you during the learning process?

Do you believe that your cell phone is a distraction for your learning?

What classroom policy regarding cell phones would you prefer?

5. Questions

Did you ask questions?

Do you believe that you should wait for a question/answer period during the class or ask questions as you go along?

6. Note taking

Did you take notes during class?

Did you feel rushed to keep up?

What are some things that could be done to help students take notes during a class activity?

7. Preparation

Did you come to class prepared?

What are some things that could be done to help students come to class prepared?

8. Participation

Did you answer any questions?

Were you called on or did you just call the answer out?

Which way do you prefer?

9. Listening skills

On a scale of 1–10 with 10 being the highest score, rank your ability to listen.

When professors give homework, which way do you prefer that they tell you the homework? Verbally? Written on a handout? Written on course website?

10. Final comment

Consider the class as a whole. How would you rank your performance (scale 1–10 with 10 being the highest score)? Please explain your ranking.

Consider the class as a whole. How would you rank the professor in his/her ability to encourage learning? Please explain your ranking.

Module 20

Reader Process

Each word below has something to do with the reading process. Define how each relates to you when you are reading textbooks. Consider how this differs from reading for pleasure.

Pace	Rereading	Planning	Analyzing	Difficulty
Length of time it takes to read	Eye movement	Unknown vocabulary	Rituals during reading	Background Information

Abandoning	Revisiting	Connecting	Rate	You

Now list the top ten things that *you want to remember* about *Reading Strategies for College and Beyond*.

The Top Ten Things from *Reading Strategies for College and Beyond*

1.

2.

3.

4.

5.

6.

7.

8.

9.

10.

Creative Strategy

This module is different than the majority of the other modules because instead of presenting a strategy for you to use, **you will create a textbook reading strategy and present it to the class.** Your textbook reading strategy should be a completely new one that you create. (In some cases, it is possible to substantively adapt one of the strategies that we've worked on in the modules, but it must be significantly different.) You will create a strategy, write it up, and present it to the class **using a format similar to those that we've used throughout the modules.** You will need to include:

Section 1.   ***Introduction.*** In this section, introduce the purpose and thoughts behind your strategy. Include the type of textbook you had in mind when creating this strategy, and how it might be adapted for different textbooks.

Section 2.   ***Step-by-Step Strategy Description.*** In this section, describe in detail how to do your strategy.

Section 3.   ***Practice Assignment and Directions.*** In this section, you need to provide an <u>excerpt from a textbook</u> and <u>instructions</u> on how to apply your strategy to that excerpt. You will demonstrate how the strategy works on a textbook excerpt with the class, and you must provide an <u>answer key</u> to the practice assignment.

Section 4.   ***Summary.*** Wrap up your strategy explanation by summarizing its key points and how it is useful.

For the Presentation:

Handout: You will need a **one-page handout** for every student in the class which includes the introduction, step-by-step instructions, and summary.

Practice Assignment Work: You will demonstrate how your strategy works with a textbook excerpt. You will need a visual aid of some sort so that all the students will be able to follow your work on the practice assignment.

Time

You will be given 5–10 minutes to demonstrate your strategy. Include the following in your demonstration:

Introduce

Explain

Work through an example

Summarize

Website Resources

There are many websites that are fun and can help you create your own presentation. Check out any site that helps you create presentations:

http://www.powtoon.com/ – create animated videos and presentations

http://prezi.com – create a presentation similar to power point but a bit more interactive

http://weebly.com – create your own website and embed any information you want

http://www.thelearnia.com – create presentations using an online whiteboard

http://www.photopeach.com – create a slideshow

http://www.stroyboardthat.com/ – create a storyboard style to present your content

http://www.myhistro.com/ – also an app; create timelines and allows for digital storytelling

Record this strategy and those of your classmates on the goal setting log on page 10–11. There are four boxes for creative strategies to be logged.

Final Note

Thoughts and reflections about future behaviors with academic textbooks

Using the format of a personal letter, write yourself a letter in the space below. (*Write reminders to yourself. Write thoughts about your behaviors with academic textbooks. Reflect on your future behaviors with academic textbooks. Include everything you wish to remember and practice. Talk to yourself in writing*) BE HONEST

Date

Dear _____
      Put your name here.

CPSIA information can be obtained
at www.ICGtesting.com
Printed in the USA
BVOW08s1801080218

507499BV00009B/207/P